HANDBOOK OF AMERICAN
SILVER AND PEWTER MARKS

Dram cup by Hull and Sanderson. This is considered one of the most important examples of the art of the silversmith in early America. (*Courtesy Mabel Brady Garvan Collection, Yale University Art Gallery*).

The famous Paul Revere Liberty Bowl, made in Boston in 1768. A superb example of the work of one of America's greatest silversmiths, it was ordered by the Sons of Liberty, a secret organization of patriots. Often called our country's "birth certificate in silver," it is now enshrined in the Boston Museum of Fine Arts. The owner, the late Mrs. J. Marsden Perry, refused offers as high as $150,000 for it. (*Courtesy Museum of Fine Arts, Boston*).

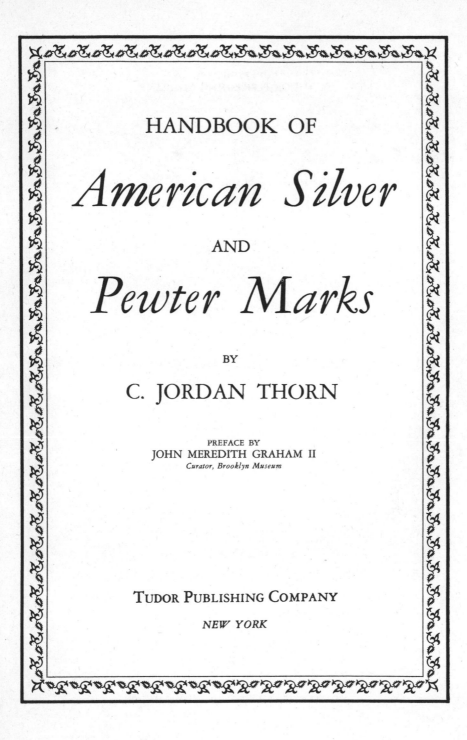

HANDBOOK OF

American Silver

AND

Pewter Marks

BY

C. JORDAN THORN

PREFACE BY
JOHN MEREDITH GRAHAM II
Curator, Brooklyn Museum

TUDOR PUBLISHING COMPANY

NEW YORK

LITHOGRAPHED IN THE UNITED STATES OF AMERICA

Preface

RECENTLY THERE HAS appeared on the American market a steady flow of books dealing with a diversity of art subjects including fine arts, decorative arts and makers' marks. Many of these publications have attained a record in sales figures for books of this type and have moved into the ranks of best sellers along with fiction.

These phenomena may partly be accounted for by a heretofore dearth of published material on subjects that general collectors have demanded. The great revival of interest in arts and crafts of the past may also be attributed to a revolt against the machine age of standardization and regimentation with the resultant loss of individuality as expressed by the artisan. Craftsmanship of the past perhaps fills this lack as no two pieces were identical. This is found to be true even in a pair of objects by the same maker where minor variations may be noted. This is especially pertinent to silversmithing, which demanded a skilled craftsman who was first required to serve an apprenticeship of seven years before he could become a master craftsman. He was his own designer as well as an artisan who was familiar with his materials and their potentialities. Deadlines, quantity, time and overtime as found in mass production were not factors to be considered as one commission might require six months or more to complete.

Silversmiths were listed among the early settlers arriving in America and their numbers increased as fortunes were made by planters, merchants and sea captains who wanted to convert their silver coins acquired from many countries into tangible assets that were useful and readily identifiable in case of theft. In the early period the colonial silversmith marked his plate with a stamp containing the first initial of his given and surname enclosed in a reserve of a heart, trefoil, shield or similar device. After 1725 the maker's given and surname began to appear as a mark, or the initial of the given name with surname was used, and as the century progressed some makers added symbols imitating English hall marks. In the 19th century the name of the place of manufacture was usually employed and later the words standard, coin, pure silver and sterling are encountered. However, exact dating of American silver within a given year is difficult due to the absence of date letters as used in the English system of marking silver.

Pewter makers, like silversmiths, arrived in America at an early date. They also were required to serve a seven year apprenticeship before becoming master craftsmen. Some of these men made both pewter and silver. Pewter, however, was not as flexible as silver and had to be cast in molds to attain its form. These molds were an expensive item for the pewterer and required a considerable outlay of capital to obtain the number necessary to produce both hollow and flatware forms. One mold was often made to serve several purposes, as exemplified by Samuel Danforth's baptismal bowls made from eight inch basins and Heyne's use of a six inch plate as a base for his flagons.

iii

American pewterers stamped a substantial part of their output with a maker's mark called a touch. These marks were of two sizes, one for larger pieces and another for small objects. A third touch was often used indicating the town.

Little is known about the early marks used by 17th century American pewterers as there is only one identified touch from Virginia which bears the name of Joseph Copeland, with the date 1675 in outer circle and the name of the town Chuckatuck and a heart in the center. The lion and unicorn, rose and crown and gateway type were used with makers initials or full name until about the time of the Revolution when the eagle touch became popular. So-called sets of hallmarks were often employed from the middle of the 18th century to the beginning of the 19th century. An X or crowned X was used to denote metal of superior quality. In the early 1800's smaller touches were employed, later followed by the maker's name in a rectangle with the letters still in relief. In the late Britannia period of the 19th century the name was marked in intaglio letters. Pewter making in this country reached impressive production figures in spite of European competition, and entered into all phases of every-day life from church use to wearing apparel. Pewter supplanted wooden ware and was in turn supplanted by mass produced glass and ceramics.

It is a rather sad commentary that American craftsmen have received such delayed recognition of their work and have had to wait until recent times for a true appreciation of their skills. The formerly magic word of "European" or "foreign," has lost its charm and has been replaced by the word "American." This is self-evident by prices now obtained in auction galleries and antique shops. Today the general collector is better informed, due to recent publications and frequent exhibitions of arts and crafts. Not only is he familiar with the various periods and style changes but he has also progressed to the finer points of distinguishing the origin of a piece by its sectional variations.

There is no truer saying than that the more a man learns the more he wants to learn. Interest in one field of collecting invariably leads to another and it is only through the knowledge of all the arts that a clear picture of American culture is possible. C. Jordan Thorn's book of 3500 American silver and pewter marks in one volume will be a welcome, inexpensive reference work for students, collectors and dealers interested in identifying the makers of their pieces in these two related subjects.

JOHN MEREDITH GRAHAM II
Curator, Brooklyn Museum

Introduction

AT FIRST IMPRESSION it may appear unusual for such diverse subjects as American silver and American pewter to be incorporated as a single topic within the covers of one book; theoretically, silver and pewter in their utilitarian forms are in some ways diametric opposites. This is similar to a discussion of early American glass and crockery as a single subject, just because they were both used as table articles in the past. However, this apparent contradiction has little foundation in actual fact. For the purposes of collecting today, the two subjects presented here are so closely related as to justify a conjugation of this nature. And, considering the fact that they are treated in separate sections, the reader will find that he has in his possession *two* books instead of one.

The markings on American silver have heretofore been considered so vast a field for study and investigation that the overwhelming majority of books on early American art consider them in the most general and cursory manner. Early American and Colonial silver and pewter (except for influences received from across the sea) developed their own forms and characteristic approaches to design and manufacture, motivated by the simplicity of the life and manners of the times. The embodiment of that feeling becomes apparent upon study of the many line drawings presented herein; at the same time, the structural similarities of much of the silver and pewter may be observed. These drawings provide an excellent key and guide to periodic design, even though specific dating on this basis alone is not ordinarily possible.

The location of these early craftsmen is indicated after each name, along with working dates and other applicable data. Naturally, in an ever-growing society, some of these artisans found themselves moving from one town to another, and in some cases these itinerant movements have been noted. The majority, however, have been listed as working in a single locality — their principal place of business; a few residential changes were too obscure or lengthy to note.

The matter of dating was a difficult one because of the profusion of material in this category. Although the dates of birth and death were known in many cases, they were omitted and the actual working dates put in their place. Fundamentally, this is what we are concerned with. Since the aim of this volume is to present information that will enable the reader to place the working years of a silversmith or pewterer as accurately as possible, we have included those dates which are most pertinent to that objective. This explains the variance in form of the matter pertaining to dating.

The dividing line between Colonial silversmiths, watchmakers and jewelers was frequently very thin. The metal silver was common to all, but the ultimate product varied. Actually, we are not concerned with either watch or jewelry making, but their association is so close that some consideration must be given to these two allied trades. References have been made by adding the letters "J" for jeweler, and "W" for watchmaker to the names of those men who carried on trade not only as silversmiths, but in these other capacities as well.

Immediately preceding the text the reader will find a key to abbreviations that will clarify their use. The text itself has been arranged in a format that subordinates every other consideration to one of utility, which, theoretically, is the purpose of this work.

C. JORDAN THORN

Contents

List of Illustrations

SECTION ONE — AMERICAN SILVER

SECTION TWO—AMERICAN PEWTER

American Silver

FROM ITS VERY INCEPTION, silversmithing in America was a highly developed trade, practiced by the most astute of craftsmen. It needed no precipitating force, no experimentation, no tedious trial and error methods such as Baron Stiegel (of Colonial glass fame) and many of our early potters were forced to contend with. America offered refuge and economic security for some of Europe's finest smiths. They brought with them to these shores the tools, the methods, and the artistic ability which were the products of generations of European culture and endeavor. Long before Gilbert Stuart, Benjamin West, and the Philadelphia cabinetmaker, William Savery, silversmithing had set its roots deep in the field of American art.

It is true that Colonial silver had but the humblest beginnings. Perhaps the superb *repoussé* work of the English Carolean period and the meticulous art of men like Paul Lamerie are lacking, but in their place we find a characteristic, utilitarian simplicity that represents a degree of perfection, both in design and decoration, that wasn't achieved elsewhere on this continent until a century later.

Teapots, porringers, candlesticks, tankards, cups and other objects for display or household use constituted the bulk of the silversmith's labors. Of course, church silver occupied a prominent place in the Colonial world. The presentation of handsome chalices and patens, beakers and flagons by well-to-do communicants was an excellent way of displaying devotion and sacrifice and of furthering the welfare of the Church. There are records indicating that as early as 1620 and 1624, the Second Church in Boston was in possession of communion silver. Unfortunately, much of our early ecclesiastical silver has been lost or destroyed, but those pieces which remain reveal a clear picture of a mode and a manner of living that has long since disappeared.

> *"A Jewellery, Silver and Plated Ware Factory is opened by Wm. Donovan, Second-street, between Walnut and Chestnut-streets, Where every article in that profession is finished in the newest and most Elegant Taste. As he has, at a considerable expence, brought experienced artists from different towns in Europe, and has all his work executed immediately under his own inspection, the Public may rely on its being faithfully and carefully put out of hands: and as the above manufactory, if attended to with industry, and properly encouraged, will be a cause of lessening the prodigious and impoverishing importations of articles in that line, Donovan most earnestly sollicits the protection and countenance of a discerning public.*
>
> *Donovan cuts . . . Office or State Seals on Metal . . . and has for sale, the new-invented Philosophic Tapers, and a most extensive assortment of Jewellery, Silver and Plated Ware."*

The above paragraphs, representing an advertisement in Carey's Penna. Evening Herald in the year 1785, proclaimed to all that one Wm. Donovan, a silversmith, was actively engaged in his trade and was prepared to fashion to the best of his ability any articles his following might desire. However, the background of that tiny advertisement is directly entwined with all the notable events and heroic achievements that comprise the basic history of this great nation.

If we were to return to the year 1700, when Boston, Massachusetts had a population of little more than 7,000, or even beyond —to the year 1650, when it was nothing more than a small, strategically located village that played host to great sailing ships from distant lands — there we would find the beginning of the American art movement. It was about this time that John Hull (1624-1683), the son of a blacksmith, was released from his gruelling apprenticeship to start out on his own in the trade of Silversmith. Hull was in all probability the first smith to learn his trade in this country, and he apparently prospered, for in 1652 he and Robert Sanderson (1608-1693) were appointed by the Massachusetts Assembly to coin the first silver money (Pine-Tree shillings) in the Colonies. This partnership worked out so well that Hull and Sanderson, in addition to acquiring wealth and political prominence, became the leading smiths of their day.

In 1659, Jeremiah Dummer (1645-1718) was apprenticed to John Hull for eight years. Shortly after attaining the rank of Freeman in 1667, he became one of the leading patriots in the Colony. Besides employing his skills at silversmithing, he held the positions of County Treasurer, Selectman, Judge and soldier. His son, William, became Lieutenant-Governor of the state. With Hull and Dummer we have the nucleus of a series of apprenticeships, marriages, and filial descendencies that eventually included, within geographical limitations, almost all of our early workers in silver.

During that period of the seventeenth century the colonists were obliged to deal with a weak paper currency that lacked a fixed valuation. This, of course, created a great demand for silver, not only as an investment but as a stable form of currency. This whole movement was directly reflected in the work of our early silversmiths, for they established the mode of "investing" their silver coin and that of their clients in the form of porringers, tankards and the like, for both immediate use and future security.

It is easy to see why the silversmith played such an important role in the life and growth of Colonial America. He was a highly skilled artisan, theoretically a banker, and in many cases a trusted civic leader. Accordingly, his position carried with it a covetous respect and prestige. Silversmithing was a skill and a tradition that was frequently and proudly handed down from generation to generation.

Versatility, often born of necessity, was a major factor in the prominence of these early artisans. John Coney (1655-1722), the brother-in-law of Jeremiah Dummer, was not only an important silversmith but a noted engraver. In 1690 he made the plates for the first paper money in America, that of Massachusetts Bay; and in 1709-13 printed the first paper money for Connecticut. Early in the eighteenth century Coney received in apprenticeship a young French immigrant, Apollos De Rivoire (1702-1754), who was later to become the father of Paul Revere, the most versatile of all our early craftsmen. De Rivoire started on his own in 1723; he flourished and eventually raised a family of twelve children. Paul Revere joined his father at the age of nineteen and rose rapidly through earnest endeavor and intelligence to become the noted artificer. Achieving immeasurable fame as a silversmith and patriot Revere was also an engraver, printer, powder manufacturer, shipbuilder, jeweler, dentist, bell-founder, brazier, ironmaster, seal maker, soldier, and politician. This imposing list of proclivities attests to the capability and ingenuity of one of our early colonists.

Silver, like furniture and architecture, was subjected to changing style. As milady's fashions changed and Queen Anne gave way to Chippendale, so the form and decoration of our early metalwork yielded to a compelling force. It was natural that the influence of the English and Dutch styles should be felt so strongly, for in the beginning it was London that supplied New England and the South; and Amsterdam that was the prime source of New York's skilled workers. However, as America grew in stature and developed its own rugged character, the handicraft of its settlers could be traced along these new lines. The lack of pretention and the simple way of life found themselves reflected in both method and design. Silver was constantly adapting itself to these changes so that the period of manufacture of many articles can be determined today by shape alone.

At times in the past there has existed a good deal of confusion over the identification of English-Irish and Dutch pieces that have American characteristics and vice-versa. This has been largely cleared up through a more accurate compilation of markings. However, in some cases a reasonable doubt still exists, for many eighteenth century Irish and Dutch pieces are marked similarly to the American. Upon examination of the maker's marks it will be observed that in this country the earliest markings followed the contemporary English custom of enclosing initials within vari-shaped devices. In the eighteenth century the initials or the surname in a plain rectangle or one of irregular lines will be found. Some English provincial and Irish makers also employed this method of marking. The words *Coin, Pure Coin, Standard, Sterling,* and *Dollar* are common on American and are infrequently found on pieces of Irish origin. To be perfectly certain of correct attribution the collector after close scrutiny must weigh the markings against form and composition.

It has not been unknown for unscrupulous persons to erase the mark of an obscure maker and place in its stead the initials or name of one of our more prominent makers such as Paul Revere. Initials alone on many pieces provide an enigma that will never be solved in entirety because the silversmith habitually used these abbreviated marks on teaspoons and other small objects. In such cases, only when sufficient proof already exists, or when initials are used in conjunction with the full name, can we definitely ascertain origin. Another problem, fortunately seldom encountered, was created by the stamping by Colonial makers of English silver that had passed through their hands. Eradication of the English marks was not difficult and care must be exercised in differentiating between English and American designs.

Silversmithing was an art that required the utmost in skill, patience, and stubborn application. After years of hard, menial work as an apprentice, the novice set out on his own, usually urged forward by economic necessity and the desire to establish a successful place for himself in the rapidly expanding community. Opportunities were abundant, so after the usual period of social and commercial adjustment the smith found easier footing and became an integral part of community life. Although the complexities of his daily tasks seemed never-ending, he approached his work with an ardor that was commonplace in Colonial times. Upon receiving from a customer a quantity of silver coins, he would first melt them down, preparatory to eliminating the impurities necessary to bring the "batch" of metal to the proper standard of .925 parts fine. (Because silver was not successfully mined in the United States until the mid-nineteenth century, South America provided the colonists with much of their early coin.) The next step was to cast the silver into a plate of necessary size and thickness preliminary to "raising." This latter process consisted of working the metal with hammer and anvil until it began to assume the requisite form. Naturally, sustained beating tended to weaken the piece so that it was frequently re-tempered to eliminate any brittleness. On close examination one can ordinarily see the hammer marks left by this operation. Occasionally the metal was drawn or "dragged" into the required proportions. This was a highly skilful maneuver that required considerable dexterity, for metal will not draw out evenly under pressure. Next, the process of soldering was employed to join finally the various parts. Decoration consisted primarily of engraving, embossing (*repoussé*), and *appliqué* work. In engraving the metal was simply cut away in narrow lines to produce the desired design, commonly an inscription or a coat of arms. Embossing is a style of ornamentation in which the pattern is worked from the inside and raised in relief. The third method was the application of additional cast silver or cut-work to the body or adjoining parts. The finished product was then stamped with the maker's mark, and, in accordance with the English custom of the day, was often incised with initials to denote ownership. In the seventeenth and eighteenth centuries these initials were in block form. The common practice for joint possession by husband and wife was to place the initial of the surname above and those of the two Christian names below as $_T{}^B{}_M$ on a porringer by John Coney made for Thomas and Mary Barton. Interlaced script letters were the predominant style in the late eighteenth and nineteenth centuries.

American silversmiths produced such a wide variety of objects that many shortly became obsolete. As America progressed so did its habits of living. Cast aside forever were such quaint articles as spout cups for feeding children and invalids; the porringer used as a taster or a serving dish; mugs, tankards, flagons, and caudle or posset cups for drinking that unusual and popular combination of wine or ale mixed with spices, sugar and bread leavings.

It was about 1742 when an impoverished cutler in Sheffield, England—Thomas Boulsover by name—accidentally discovered that a thin sheet of silver properly heated would adhere to a cheaper and more durable copper, and that the two together could be worked as one. This was truly the beginning of the quietus, for with the advent of the 19th century, Sheffield plate in conjunction with a stable economy, finally usurped the throne held so long by sterling silver.

⊰{ KEY TO ABBREVIATIONS }⊱

b. —— born
d. —— died
w. —— working
c. —— circa
(W) ——watchmaker
(J) —— jeweler
(R) —— retailer

The words "before" and "after" refer to the working period; unless otherwise noted, double dates indicate a life span.

A

AARON, JOSEPH
Philadelphia, Pa.
1798

ABBOTT, JOHN W.
Portsmouth, N. H.
1790-1850

[J.ABBOTT]

[J.W.ABBOTT]

ABBOTT, J. S.
[J.S.ABBOTT]

ACKERMAN, DAVID
New York, N. Y.
1818

ACKLEY, FRANCIS M.
New York, N. Y.
c. 1796

[F.ACKLEY] [FMA]

ACTON, GEORGE
New York, N. Y.
1795

ADAM, JOHN
Alexandria, Va.
w. 1800-1829

[JA] [JA] [JAdam]
[I.ADAM] [I·ADAM]

ADAM, JOHN B.
New Orleans, La.
1822

ADAMS, JONATHAN
Philadelphia, Pa.
1783

[ADAM] [Adam]

ADAMS, PYGAN
New London, Conn.
1712-1776

[PA] [PA] [PA]

ADAMS, R.
Early 19th Century

[R+ADAMS] [ADAMS]

ADAMS, WILLIAM L.
New York, N. Y.
w. 1831-1843
Troy, N. Y.
1844-1850

[W.ADAMS] [NEW YORK]

ADDISON, GEORGE M.
Baltimore, Md.
1804

ADGATE, WILLIAM
Norwich, Conn.
1744-1779

ADRIANCE, C. P.
[C.P.ADRIANCE]
[C.P.A]

ADRIANCE, EDWIN
St. Louis, Ill.
1809-1852

[E.ADRIANCE] [ST LOUIS]

AIKEN, GEORGE
Baltimore, Md.
1765-1832

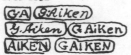

AINSWORTH, MICHAEL
Fredricksburg Co., Va.
1755

AITKEN, JOHN
Philadelphia, Pa.
w. 1785-1814

AITKINS, W
Baltimore, Md.
1802

AKERLY & BRIGGS

AKERLY & BRIGGS

AKIN, JOHN B.
Danville, Ky.
c. 1850

JOHN B. AKIN DANVILLE KY

ALDIS, CHARLES
New York, N. Y.
1814

C·ALDIS

ALEXANDER, A.
Philadelphia, Pa.
1802

ALEXANDER, ISAAC (J)
New York, N. Y.
c. 1850

I. ALEXANDER

ALEXANDER AND RIKER
New York, N. Y.
c. 1797

A & RIKER

ALEXANDER, ROBERT
Rochester, N. Y.
1825-1862

ALEXANDER & SIMMONS
Philadelphia, Pa.
1800

ALEXANDER, SAMUEL
Philadelphia, Pa.
w. 1797-1808

S·ALEXANDER

ALFORD, SAMUEL
Philadelphia, Pa.
1840

ALFORD, THOMAS
Philadelphia, Pa.
1762

ALLCOCK & ALLEN
New York, N. Y.
1820

Allcock·Allen

ALLEN & EDWARDS
Boston, Mass.
1700

IA IE

ALLEN, CHARLES
Boston, Mass.
1760

C·ALLEN

ALLEN, JAMES
Philadelphia, Pa.
1720

ALLEN, JARED T.
Rochester, N. Y.
w. 1844-1846

ALLEN, JOEL
Middletown &
Southington, Conn.
1755-1825

ALLEN, JOHN
Philadelphia, Pa.
1814

ALLEN, JOHN
Boston, Mass.
1671-1760

ALLEN, RICHARD
Philadelphia, Pa.
1816

ALLEN, ROBERT
Philadelphia, Pa.
1776

ALLEN, THOMAS
Boston, Mass.
1758

ALLISON, PETER
New York, N. Y.
1791

ALSTYNE, JERONIMUS
New York, N. Y.
w. 1787-1797

ANDERSON, WILLIAM
New York, N. Y.
w. 1724-1746

ANDRAS & CO.
New York, N. Y.
1800

ANDRAS & RICHARD
New York, N. Y.
c. 1797

ANDRAS, WILLIAM
New York, N. Y.
1795

ANDREAS, ABRAHAM
Bethlehem, Pa.
1780

ANDREW, JOHN
Salem, Mass.
1747-1791

ANDREWS, ABRAHAM
Philadelphia, Pa.
1795

ANDREWS, HENRY
Philadelphia, Pa.
1795
Boston, Mass.
1830

ANDREWS, JEREMIAH
Philadelphia, Pa.
1779

ANDREWS, JOSEPH
Norfolk, Va.
1800

ANDREWS, JR.
Philadelphia, Pa.
1746

ANDRUS, N. & CO. (W)
New York, N. Y.
1835

ANTHONY, ISAAC
Newport, R. I. & Swansea, Mass
1690-1773

ANTHONY, JOSEPH
Philadelphia, Pa.
1770

ANTHONY, JOSEPH, JR.
Philadelphia, Pa.
w. 1783-1814

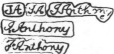

ANTHONY, JOSEPH & SONS
Philadelphia, Pa.
1810

ANTHONY, L. D.
Providence, R. I.
1805

ANTHONY, M. H. & T.
Philadelphia, Pa.
1814

ANTHONY, MICHAEL H.
Philadelphia, Pa.
1810

ANTHONY, THOMAS
Philadelphia, Pa.
1810

ANTHONY, WILLIAM
New York, N. Y.
1800

ANWYL, KENRICK
Baltimore, Md.
1780

APPLETON, GEORGE B.
Salem, Mass.
1850

[APPLETON]

ARCHIE, JOHN
New York, N. Y.
1759

ARMS, T. N.
Albany, N. Y.
1849

ARMSTRONG, ALLEN
Philadelphia, Pa.
w. 1806-1817

[A.Armstrong]
[Philadelphia]
[A.Armstrong] [Phia]

ARMSTRONG, JOHN
Philadelphia, Pa.
w. 1810-1813

ARMSTRONG, WILLIAM
Philadelphia, Pa.
1750

ARNOLD, H. B.
[H.B.Arnold.]

ARNOLD, THOMAS
Newport, R. I.
1739-1828

[T.ARNOLD] [JM]
[ARNOLD] [SA]
[TARNOLD] [TA]

ASHMEAD, WILLIAM
Philadelphia, Pa.
1797

ASKEW, JAMES
Philadelphia, Pa.
1785

ATHERTON, NATHAN
Philadelphia, Pa.
1825

ATKINSON, ISAAC
Philadelphia, Pa.
1825

ATLEE, CHARLES
Philadelphia, Pa.
1837

ATTERBURY, J.
New Haven, Conn.
1799

AUSTEN, DAVID
Philadelphia, Pa.
1837

AUSTIN, BENJAMIN
Portsmouth, N. H.
1775

AUSTIN & BOYER
Boston, Mass.
1770

[Austin]

[Boyer]

AUSTIN, EBENEZER J.
Charlestown, Mass.
Hartford, Conn. 1764
New York, N. Y. c. 1766
1733-c. 1818

[Austin]

[E·A]

[Austin]

[E.J.AUSTIN]

AUSTIN, JAMES
Charlestown, Mass.
1780

AUSTIN, JOHN
Philadelphia, Pa.
1802

AUSTIN, JOHN
Charleston, S. C.
1809-1820

AUSTIN, JOSEPH
Hartford, Conn.
1740

AUSTIN, JOSIAH
Charlestown, Mass.
1718-1780

AUSTIN, NATHANIEL
Boston, Mass.
1734-1818

AVERY, JOHN
Preston, Conn.
1732-1794

AVERY, JOHN, JR.
Preston, Conn.
1755-1815

AVERY, ROBERT S.
Preston, Conn.
1771-1846
w. until 1794

AVERY, SAMUEL
Preston, Conn.
1760-1836

AVERY, WILLIAM
Preston, Conn.
1765-1798

AVERY, W. & B.
Salisbury, N. Y.
1820

AYRES, B.

AYRES, SAMUEL
Lexington, Ky.
w. 1790-c. 1820

AYRES, T.
1800

B

BABBIT, C.
Taunton, Mass.
c. 1815

BABCOCK, SAMUEL
Saybrook, Conn.
Middletown, Conn.
1788-1857

Teapot by W. Hollingshead. (*Courtesy of Philadelphia Museum of Art*).

BACALL, THOMAS
Boston, Mass.
1836

BACHMAN, A.
New York, N. Y.
1848

BACHMAN

BACKUS, DELUCINE
New York, N. Y.
1792

D Backus   DBACKUS

DBackus

BAILEY, BENJAMIN
Boston, Mass.
1820

BAILEY, B. M.
Ludlow, Vt.
1824-1913

BMBAILEY   LUDLOW

BAILEY & CO. (J)
Philadelphia, Pa.
c. 1850

BAILEY&CO.

BAILEY, EDWARD
Baltimore, Md.
1779

BAILEY, E. E. & S. C.
Portland, Me.
1825

BAILEY, E. L. & CO.
Claremont, N. H.
1835

E.L.BAILEY &CO.

BAILEY, HENRY
Boston, Mass.
1800

HB

BAILEY, JOHN
New York, N. Y.
1762

J.Bailey

BAILEY & KITCHEN (J)
Philadelphia, Pa.
1833-46

BAILEY&KITCHEN

BAILEY, LORING
Hingham, Mass.
1780-1814

L.B

BAILEY, ROSWELL H.
Woodstock, Vt.
1825

R.H.BAILEY

BAILEY, SIMEON A.
New York, N. Y.
1789

BAILEY, WILLIAM
Utica, N. Y.
c. 1818

W.BAILEY

BAILY, W. JR. (W)
Philadelphia, Pa.
w: 1816-1822

W.BAILY Jr.

BAILY, WM. (W)

Philadelphia, Pa.
c. 1820-1850

[WBAILY]

BAKER

Boston, Mass.
1765

BAKER, ANSON

New York, N. Y.
1821

BAKER, E. (W)

New York, N. Y.
1740-1790

[E.BAKER]

BAKER, ELEAZER

Ashford, Conn.
1764-1849

[E·BAKER]

BAKER, GEORGE

Providence, R. I.
1823

[G.BAKER] [G.BAKER]

BAKER, STEPHEN

New York, N. Y.
1787-1853

[S.BAKER] ⠿

BALCH, EBENEZER

Hartford, Conn. 1744
Wethersfield, Conn., after 1756
1723-1808

[E.BALCH]

BALCH & FRYER

Albany, N. Y.
1784

BALDWIN & BAKER

Providence, R. I.
1817

BALDWIN & CO.

Newark, N. J.
1830

[BALDWIN&CO] [NEWARK]

BALDWIN, EBENEZER

Hartford, Conn.
w. 1810-1819

[BALDWIN] [BALDWIN.]

BALDWIN, H. E. & CO. (R)

New Orleans, La.
1825

[H.E. BALDWIN & Co.]
[NEW ORLEANS]

BALDWIN, JABEZ C.

Boston, Mass.
1777-1819

BALDWIN

JCBALDWIN

BALDWIN AND STORRS

Northampton, Mass.
1792-1794

[J.&S. BALDWIN]

BALDWIN, JEDEDIAH (W)

Northampton, Mass., 1791
Hanover, N. H., 1793
Rochester, N. Y., 1834
1768-1849

[J.BALDWIN]

[I.BALDWIN]

BALDWIN & JONES
Boston, Mass.
1813

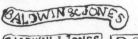

BALDWIN, STANLEY S. (J) (W)
New York, N. Y.
1820

BALL, BLACK & CO. (J)
New York, N. Y.
1851-1876

BALL & HEALD
Baltimore, Md.
c. 1810

BALL, DAVID
Rochester, N. Y.
c. 1845

BALL, HENRY
New York, N. Y.
1833

BALL, JOHN
Boston, Mass.
c. 1765

BALL, SHELDON
Buffalo, N. Y.
w. 1821-1836

BALL, S. S.
Boston, Mass.
1833

BALL, TOMKINS & BLACK (J)
New York, N. Y.
1839-1851

BALL, TRUE M.
Boston, Mass.
1815-1890

BALL, WILLIAM, JR.
Baltimore, Md.
w. 1785-1815

BALL, WILLIAM
Philadelphia, Pa.
w. 1759-1771

BANCKER, ADRIAN
New York, N. Y.
1703-1772

BANGS, JOHN J.
Cincinnati, O.
c. 1825

BARBERET, THEON
New Orleans, La.
1822

BARBIER, PETER
Philadelphia, Pa.
1823

BARD, CONRAD
    Philadelphia, Pa.
    w. 1825-1850

C.BARD 2ᵈˢ ARCH ST.

C.BARD

BARD, C. & SON
    Philadelphia, Pa.
    1850

BARD & HOFFMAN
    Philadelphia, Pa.
    1837

BARD, J.
    Philadelphia, Pa.
    1800

BARD & LAMONT
    Philadelphia, Pa.
    1841

BARD & LAMONT

BARDEER, CUNNARD
    Philadelphia, Pa.
    1831

BARDICK, GEORGE
    Philadelphia, Pa.
    1790

G.B

BARDICK, JOHN
    Philadelphia, Pa.
    1805

BARDON, STEPHEN
    Philadelphia, Pa.
    1785

BARIA, WILLIAM
    New York, N. Y.
    1805

BARKER AND MUMFORD
    Newport, R. I.
    1825

BARKER & MUMFORD

BARNES, ABRAHAM
    Boston, Mass.
    1716

BARON, LOUIS
    Rochester, N. Y.
    w. 1862-1867

BARRET, JAMES
    Norwich, Conn.
    1717

JB

BARRETT, JAMES
    New York, N. Y.
    1805

BARRETT, JOSEPH
    Nantucket, Mass.
    w. 1753

J.BARRETT

BARRETT, SAMUEL
    Nantucket, Mass.
    c. 1780

S.BARRETT

★ S.BARRETT ★

BARRIERE, DAVID
    Baltimore, Md.
    c. 1810

D.BARRIERE

BARRINGTON & DAVENPORT
Philadelphia, Pa.
1806

[B&D]

BARROWS, JAMES M.
Tolland, Conn.
b 1809, w.c. 1828

[J.M.BARROWS]

BARRY, STANDISH
Baltimore, Md.
1763-1844

[Standish] [Barry]

[Standish] [Barry]

[Barry] [1792]

[SB] [SB] [SB] [BARRY]

BARTHOLOMEW, JOSEPH
Philadelphia, Pa.
1833

BARTHOLOMEW, LEROUX
New York, N. Y.
1688-1713

[BR]

BARTHOLOMEW, ROSWELL
Hartford, Conn.
1781-1830

[RB]

BARTLETT, EDWARD
Philadelphia, Pa.
1833

BARTLETT, ISRAEL
Newbury, Mass.
Haverhill, Mass.
1748-1838

[I.BARTLET]

BARTLETT, NATHANIEL
Concord, Mass.
1760

[N·BARTLETT]

BARTLETT, SAMUEL
Boston, Mass.
1750-1821

[J.B] [S·BARTLETT]

BARTON, B.

[B.BARTON]

BARTON, ERASTUS
New York, N. Y.
1810

BARTON, ERASTUS, & CO.
New York, N. Y.
1821

[EB&CO]

BARTON, JOSEPH
Stockbridge, Mass.
Utica, N. Y. from 1804
1764-1832

[J.BARTON]

BARTON, WILLIAM
Philadelphia, Pa.
1769

BARTRAM, WILLIAM
Philadelphia, Pa.
1769

[WB]

BASSETT, FRANCIS
New York, N. Y.
1774

[BASSETT]

1700   1720   1800

1770   1780   1790

1750   1790   1760

1800   1730   1815

BASSETT & WARFORD
Albany, N. Y.
1806

BASSETT & WARFORD

ALBANY

BATCHELLOR, N.
New York, N. Y.
1825

BATTEL, A. T.
Utica, N. Y.
1847

A.T.BATTEL   UTICA

BAY, A. S.
New York, N. Y.
1786

BAYEUX, HENRY
Troy, N. Y.
w. 1801-1812

BAYEUX

BAYLEY, ALEXANDER
New York, N. Y.
1790

BAYLEY & DOUGLAS
New York, N. Y.
1798

DB&AD

BAYLEY, JOHN
Philadelphia, Pa.
1754-1783

IB

BAYLEY, S. & A.
New York, N. Y.
1790

BAYLEY, SIMON A.
New York, N. Y.
1789

BAYLEY   BAYLEY

BAYNES, ROBERT. B. (W)
Nantucket, Mass.
1841

BAYSSET, JOSEPH
New Orleans, La.
1822

BEACH, A.
Hartford, Conn.
1823

A.BEACH

BEACH, ISAAC
New Milford, Conn.
1788

BEACH, IVES & CO.
New York, N. Y.
1820

BEACH, MILES
Litchfield, Conn.
1742-1828

MB   M.B   BEACH

BEACH & SANFORD
Hartford, Conn.
c. 1785

B&S   B&S

BEACH & WARD
Hartford, Conn.
c. 1789

B&W

one large spoon

BEAL, CALEB
Boston, Mass.
1746-1801

BEAM, JACOB C.
Philadelphia, Pa.
1818

BEARD, B. E.
Philadelphia, Pa.
c. 1800

BEARD, DUNCAN
Delaware
w.c. 1765

DB

BEATTY, G.

G.BEATTY

BEAU, JOHN A.
Philadelphia, Pa.
1772

BEAUVAIS, E. A.
St. Louis, Mo.
c. 1840

E.A.BEAUVAIS

BEAUVAIS, RENO
St. Louis, Mo.
1850

R BEAUVAIS ST LOUIS

BECHAM
c. 1740

BECHAM

BECK, THOMAS
Philadelphia, Pa., 1774
Trenton, N. J., 1784

BECKER, FREDERICK
New York, N. Y.
1736

BECKER, PHILLIP
Lancaster, Pa.
1764

PB

BEDFORD, JOHN
Fishkill, N. Y.
1757-1834

BEEBE, JAMES W.
New York, N. Y.
1835

J.W.BEEBE

BEEBE, J. W. & CO.
New York, N. Y.
1844

J.W.BEEBE&CO

BEEBE, STANTON
Providence, R. I.
1824

BEEBE, WILLIAM
New York, N. Y.
1850

BEEBE

BEECHER, CLEMENT
Berlin, Conn.
Cheshire, Conn. from 1818
1778-1869

CB

BEECHER C. & CO.
Meriden, Conn.
1820

BELIN, LEWIS
Philadelphia, Pa.
1818

BELKNAP, SAMUEL
Boston, Mass.
1789

BELL, JOSEPH (W)
New York, N. Y.
w. 1817-1824

BELL, S. W. (W)
Philadelphia, Pa.
1837

✳ | S. BELL. | ✳

BELLIARD, FRANCOIS
New Orleans, La.
1822

BELLONI, LOUIS J.
New York, N. Y.
1835

BELLONI & DURANDEAU
New York, N. Y.
1835

BEMENT, B.
Pittsfield, Mass.
1810
| B.BEMENT |

BENEDICT, J.
New York, N. Y.
1830

BENEDICT, ANDREW C. (W)
New York, N. Y.
1840
A.C.BENEDICT.

BENEDICT & SON
New York, N. Y.
1840

BENEDICT & SQUIRE (W)
New York, N. Y.
1839
| BENEDICT & SQUIRE |

BENJAMIN, BARZILLAI
New Haven, Conn.
Bridgeport, Conn.
1774-1844
| BB | | B.BENJAMIN |

BENJAMIN, BENJAMIN
New York, N. Y.
1825
| B.B | | B.BENJAMIN |

BENJAMIN, EVERARD
New Haven, Conn.
1807-1874
| E.BENJAMIN |

BENJAMIN, E. & CO.
New Haven, Conn.
c. 1830-1840
E.BENJAMIN & Cº
| EB&Cº |

BENJAMIN, JOHN
Stratford, Conn.
1730-1796
| J.B | | I.B |

BENJAMIN, SAMUEL C.
New Haven, Conn.
1801-1831

BENJAMIN, SOLOMON
Baltimore, Md.
1817

BENNET, JAMES
New York, N. Y.
1773

BENNETT, JACOB
Philadelphia, Pa.
1839

BENTLEY, THOMAS
Boston, Mass.
1764-1804

BENTSON, PETER
Philadelphia, Pa.
1718

BERARD, E.
Philadelphia, Pa.
1797
EBERARD

BERING, JOHN
Charleston, S. C.
c. 1790-1807

BERKENBUSH, CHARLES H.
New York, N. Y.
1825

BERRY, WILLIAM
New York, N. Y.
1805

BESLEY, THAUVET
New York, N. Y.
w. 1727, d. 1757

BESSAR, H. W.
H:W.BESSAR

BESSELIEVRE, THOMAS
Philadelphia, Pa.
1831

BEST, JOSEPH
Philadelphia, Pa.
1723

BEST, ROBERT
Cincinnati, O.
w. 1817

BEVAN, RICHARD
Baltimore, Md.
1804

BICKNELL, FRANCIS
Rome, N. Y.
w. 1819
F. BICKNELL

BIERSHING, HENRY
Hagerstown, Md.
w. 1815-1843
HB

BIGELOW & BROS.
Boston, Mass.
1840
BIGELOW&BROTHERS

BIGELOW BROS. & KENNARD
Boston, Mass.
1845
BIGELOW BROS & KENNARD

BIGELOW, JOHN
Boston, Mass.
1830

JOHN BIGELOW

BIGGS, JOSEPH
New York, N. Y.
1830

BIGOTUT, S.
New York, N. Y.
1800

BIJOTAL, SILVIAN A.
New York, N. Y.
1795

BILLINGS, ANDREW
Poughkeepsie, N. Y.
w. 1784-1810

A BILLINGS AB ✦

BILLINGS, A.
Preston, Conn.
1780

A.BILLINGS A.BILLING
A.B ◄·A·JJ·4·2·0·J

BILLINGS, DANIEL
Preston, Conn.
1795

D. Billings

BILLON, CHARLES
St. Louis, Mo.
1821

C BILLON

BINGHAM, JOHN
Newark, N. J.
1664

BINNEAU, THEODORE
Philadelphia, Pa.
1820

BIRD, CONARD
Philadelphia, Pa.
1831

BIRD, JOHN S.
Charleston, S. C.
w. 1820 c. 1861

JS BIRD

BIRD, JOSEPH

JOSEPH BIRD

BISSBROWN, THOMAS
Albany, N. Y.
1790

BIXLER, CHRISTIAN
Easton, Pa.
1784

BLACK, JAMES (J)
Philadelphia, Pa.
w. 1795-1819

J.B I·BLACK

BLACK, JOHN
Philadelphia, Pa.
1819

J.B

BLACK, WILLIAM
New York, N. Y.
1833

BLACKMAN, FREDERICK S.
Danbury, Conn.
1811-1898

F.S.BLACKMAN F.S.B.Co

Top: teapot with wooden handle, c. 1750, maker unknown. Center: globular teapot by Josiah Austin, 1760-1775. Bottom: pear-shaped teapot by Joseph Edwards, Jr., 1760-1775. (*Courtesy of The Metropolitan Museum of Art*).

BLACKMAN, JOHN C.
Danbury, Conn.
Bridgeport, Conn.
1808-1872

> J.C.B.B Cº
> BRIDGEPORT

BLACKMAN, JOHN S.
Danbury, Conn.
1777-1851

> J.SB

BLAKSLEE, WILLIAM
Newtown, Conn.
1795-1879

BLAKSLEE, ZIBA
Newtown, Conn.
1768-1825

BLANCHARD, ASA
Lexington, Ky.
w.c. 1810. d. 1838

> A.BLANCHARD
> A.BLANCHARD

BLANCK, JURIAN
New York, N. Y.
b.c. 1645

> IB

BLAUVELT, JOHN W.
New York, N. Y.
1835

BLEASOM & REED
Portsmouth, N. H.
1830

> BLEASOM& REED NASSAU

BLISS, JONATHAN
Middletown, Conn.
1800

> J.BLISS

BLONDELL, ANTHONY
Philadelphia, Pa.
1797

BLONDELL & DESCURET
Philadelphia, Pa.
1798

BLOWERS, JOHN
Boston, Mass.
1710-1748

BOCK, JOSEPH
Charleston, S. C.
1859-1891

BOEHLER, ANDREAS W.
New York, N. Y.
1784

BOEHME, CHARLES L.
Baltimore, Md.
1774-1868

BOELEN, HENRICUS
New York, N. Y.
1684-1755

BOELEN, JACOB
New York, N. Y.
1657-1729

BOELEN, JACOB, II
New York, N. Y.
1733-1786

BOELEN, JACOB, III
New York, N. Y.
1785

BOEMPER, ABRAHAM
Bethlehem, Pa.
1780

BOGARDUS, EVERADUS
New York, N. Y.
c. 1700

BOGERT, ALBERT
New York, N. Y.
1815

BOGERT, NICHOLAS J.
New York, N. Y.
w. 1801-1830

N·BOGERT N.J.BOGERT

BOLTON, JAMES
New York, N. Y.
1789

BOND, W.
c. 1765
W·Bond

BONJEAN, VICTOR
New Orleans, La.
1822

BONNET, JAMES
New York, N. Y.
1769

BONTECOU, TIMOTHY
New Haven, Conn.
1693-1784

 T.B. TB.

BONTECOU, TIMOTHY, JR.
New Haven, Conn.
1723-1789

TB

BOONE, JEREMIAH
Philadelphia, Pa.
1791

J·BOONE

BOOTH, EZRA B.
Rochester, N. Y.
1805-1888

E·B·BOOTH

BORDEAUX, AUGUSTINE
Philadelphia, Pa.
1793

BORHEK, E.
Philadelphia, Pa.
1835

E·BORHEK STANDARD

BOSS & KINDELL
New York, N. Y.
1794

BOSTWICK, ZALMON
New York, N. Y.
1846

Z.BOSTWICK

BOSWORTH, SAMUEL
Buffalo, N. Y.
w. 1816-1837

BOSWORTH

BOTSFORD, GIDEON B.
Woodbury, Conn.
1776-1866

G.B.BOTSFORD

BOUDAR, JOSEPH
New York, N. Y.
1800

BOUDINOT, ELIAS
Philadelphia, Pa.
1706-1770

BOUDINOT

EB BOUDINOT

BOUDO, HELOISE
Charleston, S. C.
w. 1827-1837

BOUDO, LOUIS
Charleston, S. C.
w.c. 1809-1827

L:BOUDO

BOULLIEN, MOUSIER
Philadelphia, Pa.
1811

BOURDET, STEPHEN
New York, N. Y.
1730

SB

BOUTIER, JOHN (J)
New York, N. Y.
1805

J.BOUTIER

BOUTELLE, JAMES
Worcester, Mass.
1787

BOUVAR, JOSEPH
Philadelphia, Pa.
1797

BOUVIER, DANIEL
Putnam, O.
w. 1816

BOWER, C.
Philadelphia, Pa.
1831

BOWER

BOWMAN, ELIAS
Rochester, N. Y.
c. 1834

E.BOWMAN

BOWNE, SAMUEL
New York, N. Y.
1773

S:BOWNE   SBOWNE

BOYCE, GERADUS
New York, N. Y.
1814

G.B   G:BOYCE

G.BOYCE

BOYCE & JONES
New York, N. Y.

B&J.   BOYCE&JONES

BOYCE, JARED
New York, N. Y.
1820

BOYCE, JOHN
New York, N. Y.
1801

J.B

BOYD & HOYT
Albany, N. Y.

BOYD, JOSEPH W.
New York, N. Y.
1820

J.W.B

BOYD & MULFORD
Albany, N. Y.
1832-1842

BOYD, WILLIAM
Albany, N. Y.
1800

BOYER & AUSTIN
Boston, Mass.
1770

BOYER, DANIEL
Boston, Mass.
1726 1779

D·B   DB   BOYER
Boyer   BOYER

BOYER, JAMES
Boston, Mass.
1700-1741
1830

BOYLSTON, E.
Stockbridge, Mass.
1789

BRABANT, ISAAC
Savannah, Ga.
1750

BRACKETT, JEFFREY R.
Boston, Mass.
1840

JEFFREY R. BRACKETT

BRADBURY, THEOPHILUS
Newburyport, Mass.
1815

BRADBURY   Bradbury

BRADBURY & BROTHER
Newburyport, Mass.
1810

BRADFORD, CHARLES H.
Westerly, R. I.

BRADLEY, ABNER
New Haven, Conn.
1753-1824

A. BRADLEY

BRADLEY & BUNCE
Hartford, Conn.
1830

BRADLEY, H. G.
Mantua, N. H.
c. 1815-1830

BRADLEY, LUTHER
New Haven, Conn.
1772-1830

L·B

BRADLEY & MERRIMAN
New Haven, Conn.
1826-1847

B & M

BRADLEY, PHINEAS
New Haven, Conn.
1745-1797

PB PB

BRADLEY, RICHARD
Hartford, Conn.
1787-1867

BRADLEY, ZEBUL
New Haven, Conn.
1780-1859

Z.BRADLEY

BRADY, E.
New York, N. Y.
1825

BRADY E.BRADY

BRADY, WM. V.
New York, N. Y.
1835

BRAINARD, CHARLES
Hartford, Conn.
1787-1850

BRAMHALL, S.
Plymouth, Mass.
1800

S.BRAMHALL

BRANDT, A. & C.
Philadelphia, Pa.
1800

A&C.BRANDT

BRASHER (BRASIER), AMABLE
New York, N. Y.
Philadelphia, Pa.
w. 1790-1828

A.BRASIER

BRASHER & ALEXANDER
New York, N. Y.
1800

BRASHER, E. & CO.
New York, N. Y.
1790

EB&CO.

BRASHER, EPHRAIM
New York, N. Y.
w.c. 1786-1805

EB EB E.BRASHER

BRASHER

BRAY, HENRY
Philadelphia, Pa.
1799

BREED, JOHN
Colchester, Conn.
1752-1803

BREED, WILLIAM
Boston, Mass.
1750

 WB WB M3reed

BRENTON, BENJAMIN
New York, N. Y.
1695-1749

BB BB BB

BREVOORT, JOHN
New York, N. Y.
1715-1775

 IBV. IBV IBV

BREWER, CHARLES
Middletown, Conn.
1778-1860

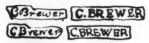

BREWER & CO.
Middletown, Conn.
1810

BREWER & MANN
Middletown, Conn.
1805

BREWSTER, ABEL
Norwalk, Conn.
1797

BRIDGE, JOHN
Boston, Mass.
w. 1723, w. 1751

BRIGDEN, C.
Boston, Mass.
1770

BRIGDEN, ZECHARIAH
Boston, Mass.
1734-1787

BRIGDEN, TIMOTHY
Albany, N. Y.
1774-1819

BRIGHT, ANTHONY
Philadelphia, Pa.
1739

BRINDSMAID, ABRAHAM
Burlington, Vt.
1815

BRINDSMAID & HILDRETH
Burlington, Vt.
1830

BRINKLEY, WILLIAM
New York, N. Y.
1802

BRINTON, GORDON & QUIRK
Boston, Mass.
1780

BRITTON, ISAAC
Philadelphia, Pa.
1811

BRITTON, JACOB
Philadelphia, Pa.
1807

BROADHURST, SAMUEL
New York, N. Y.
1725

BROCK, JOHN (J)
New York, N. Y.
1833

| J.BROCK |

| 72 CHATHAM ST |

| I.BROCK . NEW YORK |

BROCK, L.
New York, N. Y.
1830

| L.BROCK |

BROOKHOUSE, ROBERT
Salem, Mass.
b. 1779, w. to 1819

BROOKS, NICHOLAS
Philadelphia, Pa.
1775

BROOKS, SAMUEL
Philadelphia, Pa.
1793

| BRooks |

BROTHEARS, MICHAEL
Philadelphia, Pa.
1772

BROWER & RUSHER
New York, N. Y.
1834

| B&R |

BROWER, S. & B.
Albany, N. Y.
1810-c. 1850

| S&B.BROWER |

BROWER, S. DOUGLAS
Troy, N. Y.
Albany, N. Y.
w.c. 1832-1850

BROWER, WALTER S.
Albany, N. Y.
1850

BROWN, ALEXANDER
Philadelphia, Pa.
1840

BROWN, CHARLES C.
Rochester, N. Y.
1827-1871

BROWN, D .
Philadelphia, Pa.
1811

| D.BROWN |

BROWN, EBENEZER
Boston, Mass.
1793

BROWN, ELNATHAN C.
Westerly, R. I.

BROWN, HENRY
Philadelphia, Pa.
1777

BROWN & HOULTON
Baltimore, Md.
1799

BROWN, JAMES
Philadelphia, Pa.
1785

1680   1690   1700   1710

1710   1720   1740   1760

1775   1800   1820

1780   1790   1760

1710   1730   1770

BROWN, JESSE
Philadelphia, Pa.
1813

BROWN, JOHN
Philadelphia, Pa.
w. 1785-1824

J.B

BROWN, L.
Rochester, N. Y.
c. 1838

BROWN, LIBERTY
Philadelphia, Pa.
w. 1801-1819

L Brown

BROWN, R. J. & SON
Boston, Mass.
After 1833

R.BROWN & SON

BROWN, ROBERT J.
Boston, Mass.
After 1813

ROBERT J. BROWN.

BROWN, R. R.
Baltimore, Md.
1813-1830

RBROWN R.BROWN
RBROWN 10 CT 15
see Eneko

BROWN, S. (W)
New York, N. Y.
c. 1815-1820

BROWN, S. D.
Albany, N. Y.
1834

BROWN, SAMUEL C.
New York, N. Y.
c. 1825

S.BROWN S.BROWN

BROWN, SETH E.
c. 1850

Seth E. Brown

SETH E. BROWN

BROWN, WILLIAM
Albany, N. Y.
1849

W. BROWN

BROWN, WILLIAM
Baltimore, Md.
1810

Wᵐ BROWN

BROWN & KIRBY
New Haven, Conn.
c. 1850

BROWN & KIRBY

BROWNE, LIBERTY
Philadelphia, Pa.
1801

BROWNE & SEAL
Philadelphia, Pa.
1810

BROWNE & SEAL

BRUFF, CHARLES O.
New York, N. Y.
w.c. 1763-1783

 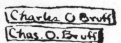

BRUFF, JOSEPH
Easton, Md.
1730-1785

BRUFF, THOMAS
Easton, Md.
1790

BRUSH, EDWARD
New York, N. Y.
1774

BRYAN, PHILLIP
Philadelphia, Pa.
1802

[BRYAN]

BUCHE, PETER
New York, N. Y.
1795

BUCHOZ, I. R.
New York, N. Y.
1835

BUCK, AZARIAH
Rochester, N. Y.
w. 1847-1850

BUCKLEY & ANDERSON
Philadelphia, Pa.
1804

BUCKLEY, J. B.
Philadelphia, Pa.
1807

[BUCKLEY]

BUDDY, DANIEL
Philadelphia, Pa.
1769

BUEL, ABEL
New Haven, Conn.
Hartford, Conn.
1742-1825

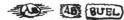

BUEL, D. H.
Hartford, Conn.
1825

BUEL & GREENLEAF
New Haven, Conn.
1798

BUEL, JOHN
New Haven, Conn.
1744-1783

BUEL & MIX
New Haven, Conn.
1783

BUEL, SAMUEL
Middletown, Conn.
1742-1819

[S·B]

BUICHLE, LEWIS
Baltimore, Md.
1798

BULL, CALEB
Hartford, Conn.
1746-1797

BULL, EPAPHRAS
Boston, Mass.
1813

BULL, G. W.
E. Hartford, Conn.
1840

G.W.BULL

BULL, MARTIN
Farmington, Conn.
1744-1825

BULL & MORRISON
Hartford, Conn.
1780

BULLES & CHILDS
Hartford, Conn.
1840

BULLES & CHILDS
HARTFORD

BULY, JOHN
Philadelphia, Pa.
1778

BUMM, PETER
Philadelphia, Pa.
1814

BUMM & SHEPPER
Philadelphia, Pa.
1819

BUMM &
SHEPPER

BUNKER, BENJAMIN
Nantucket, Mass.
1751-1842

BB   BB

BURBANK, A. F.
Worcester, Mass.
1845

A.F.BURBANK
A.F.B   BOSTON

BURDICK, WILLIAM S.
New Haven, Conn.
1810

BURDOCK, GEORGE
Philadelphia, Pa.
1791

BURDOCK, NICHOLAS
Philadelphia, Pa.
1797

N·B

BURGALIE, J. P.
New York, N. Y.
1799

BURGER, DAVID I.
New York, N. Y.
1805

D·I·Burger

BURGER, JOHN
New York, N. Y.
w. 1786-1807

I·B   BURGER

The Hartt Tea Set by Paul Revere. The engraved inscription on the sugar bowl on the right reads, "To Edmund Hartt Constructor of the Frigate BOSTON. Presented by a number of his fellow citizens, as a memorial of their sense of his Ability, Zeal, & Fidelity in the completion of that Ornament of the American Navy, 1799." (*Courtesy Museum of Fine Arts, Boston*).

BURGER, JOHN
New York, N. Y.
w. 1767-c. 1795

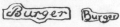
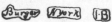

BURGER, THOMAS
New York, N. Y.
1805

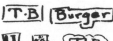

BURNAP, DANIEL
East Windsor, Conn.
1760-1838

BURNAP, ELA (W)
Boston, Mass., 1810
New York, N. Y., 1817
Rochester, N. Y., 1825
1784-1856

BURNET, SAMUEL
Newark, N. J.
1796

BURNETT, CHARLES A.
Alexandria, Va.
1793

BURNETT & RYDER
Philadelphia, Pa.
1795

BURNHAM, ROBERT
New York, N. Y.
1790

BURKLOE, SAMUEL
Philadelphia, Pa.
1795

BURNS, ANTHONY
Philadelphia, Pa.
1785

BURNS, JAMES
Philadelphia, Pa.
1810

BURNS, JOHN H.
New York, N. Y.
1835

BUROT, ANDREW
Baltimore, Md.
1819

BURR, ALBERT C.
Rochester, N. Y.
1806-1832

BURR, ALEXANDER J.
Rochester, N. Y.
c. 1835

BURR, CHRISTOPHER A.
Providence, R. I.
1810

BURR, CORNELIUS A.
Rochester, N. Y.
1816-1863

BURR, C. A., & CO.
Rochester, N. Y.
c. 1850-1864

BURR, E. & W.
Providence, R. I.
1793

BURR, EZEKIEL
Providence, R. I.
1765-1846

BURR & LEE
Providence, R. I.
1815

BURR, NATHANIEL
Fairfield, Conn.
1698-1784

BURR, WILLIAM
Providence, R. I.
1793

BURRILL, JOSEPH
Boston, Mass.
1823

BURRILL, SAMUEL
Boston, Mass.
1733

BURRILL, SAMUEL, JR.
Boston, Mass.
1820

BURRILL, THEOPHILUS
Boston, Mass.
New London, Conn.
d. 1739

BURROWS, WILLIAM
Philadelphia, Pa.
1831

BURT, BENJAMIN
Boston, Mass.
1729-1805

BURT, JOHN
Boston, Mass.
1691-1745

BURT, SAMUEL
Boston, Mass.
1724-1754

BURT, WILLIAM
Boston, Mass.
1726-1752

Left: coffee pot by Pygan Adams; Right: late 18th Century coffee pot with corkscrew thumbpiece, unidentified "HM" mark. (*Courtesy of The Metropolitan Museum of Art*).

Chocolate pot by Edward Winslow. Fluted base, duck-necked spout, domed cover, removable cap and acorn finial are typical of late 17th and early 18th Century. (*Courtesy of The Metropolitan Museum of Art*)

BURTON, JACOB
Philadelphia, Pa.
1839

F. W. BURWELL

F.W. BURWELL

G. BUSH

G.BUSH

BUSHNELL, PHINEAS
Guilford, Conn.
1762

BUSSEY, BENJAMIN
Dedham, Mass.
1757-1842

BB   BB

BUSSEY, THOMAS D.
Baltimore, Md.
1773-1804

TD Bufy

BUSWELL, JASON
Portsmouth, N. H.
1839

BUTLER, CHARLES P.
Charleston, S. C.
w.c. 1790-1852

CPB

BUTLER, HENRY W.
Philadelphia, Pa.
1833

BUTLER, JAMES
Boston, Mass.
1713-1776

IB   IB   JBUTLER
J.BUTLER

BUTLER, JOHN
Portland, Me.
1765

BUTLER, N.
Utica, N. Y.
c. 1800

BUTLER, N. H.
Philadelphia, Pa.
1837

BUTLER & LITTLE
Portland, Me.
1759

BUTLER & McCARTY
Philadelphia, Pa.
c. 1850

BUTLER & McCARTY

BUTLER, WISE & CO.
Philadelphia, Pa.
1845

BW&C°

BUZELL, J. L.
c. 1750

J.L.BUZELL

BYRD, WILLIAM
Charleston, S. C.
1802

BYRNE, JAMES
Philadelphia, Pa., 1784
New York, N. Y., 1789

BYRNES, THOMAS
Wilmington, Del.
c. 1790

CAMOIN
Philadelphia, Pa.
1797

CAMP, ELIAS
Bridgeport, Conn.
1825

C

CADY, SAMUEL
New York, N. Y.
1792

CADY & BACKUS
New York, N. Y.
1792

CAIRNS, JOHN
Rochester, N. Y.
c. 1827

CALDER & CO.
Albany, N. Y.
1830

CALDWELL, E.
New York, N. Y.
1800

CALDWELL, JAMES E. (J)
Philadelphia, Pa.
w. 1836-1842

CAMERON (CAMMAN),
ALEXANDER
Albany, N. Y., 1813

CAMPBELL, CHRISTOPHER
New York, N. Y.
1808

CAMPBELL, JOHN
Fayetteville, N. C.
1829

CAMPBELL, JOHN W.
New York, N. Y.
1814

CAMPBELL, R. & A.
Baltimore, Md.
c. 1850

CAMPBELL, ROBERT
Baltimore, Md.
1799-1872

CAMPBELL, THOMAS
New York, N. Y., 1800
Philadelphia, Pa., 1828

CAMPBELL, WILLIAM
Carlisle, Pa.
1765

CANAVILLO, ANTONIO
New York, N. Y.
1825

CANAVILLO, S.
New York, N. Y.
1825

CANDEE, L. B. & CO.
Woodbury, Conn.
1830
L.B CANDEE & CO

CANDEE, LEWIS B.
Woodbury, Conn.
1806-1861

CANDELL, CHARLES
New York, N. Y.
1795
CC

CANFIELD & BROTHER
Baltimore, Md.
1830

CANFIELD & FOOT
Middletown, Conn.
1798

CANFIELD & HALL
New York, N. Y.
1805
CANFIELD & HALL

CANFIELD, SAMUEL
Middletown, Conn.
w.c. 1780-1800
Lansingburg, N. Y., 1801
CANFIELD

CANFIELD BROTHERS & CO.
Baltimore, Md.
1850

CANN, JOHN
New York, N. Y.
1835

CANON (CANNON), GEORGE
Nantucket, Mass.
1767-1835
GC GCANON

CANT, GODFREY
New York, N. Y.
1796

CAPELLE, J.
St. Louis, Mo.
1850
CAPELLE ST LOUIS

CARALIN, PIERCE
New York, N. Y.
1804

CARBIN, THEODORUS
Philadelphia, Pa.
1758-1775

CARIO, MICHAEL
New York, N. Y.
1728

CARIO, WILLIAM
New York, N. Y.
b. 1721, w. 1760
W.CARIO W.CARIO

CARIOLLE
New Orleans, La.
1822

CARLETON & KIMBALL

CARLETON & KIMBALL

CARLETON, GEORGE
New York, N. Y.
1810

CARLETON

CARLISLE, ABRAHAM
Philadelphia, Pa.
c. 1780

A. Carlisle

CARMAN, JOHN
Philadelphia, Pa., 1771
New York, N. Y., 1800

IC

CARMAN, SAMUEL
New York, N. Y.
1807

CARON, NICHOLAS
New York, N. Y.
1718

CARPENTER, CHARLES
Boston, Mass.
1807

CC

CARPENTER, JOSEPH
Norwich, Conn.
1747-1804

I·C IC I·C

CARRELL, DANIEL
Philadelphia, Pa.
Before 1790
Charleston, S. C.
w. 1790-c. 1801

CARRELL, JOHN & DANIEL
Philadelphia, Pa.
1784

CARREL

CARRIBEC, PETER
Philadelphia, Pa.
1795

CARRINGTON, WILLIAM
Charleston, S. C.
1830

W.CARRINGTON

CARROL, JAMES
Albany, N. Y.
1834

CARROLL, JAMES
New York, N. Y.
1825

CARSON, DAVID
Albany, N. Y.
1849

CARSON, THOMAS
Albany, N. Y.
1815

TC

CARSON & HALL
Albany, N. Y.
1813

Carson & Hall

CART, JOSEPH S.
Charleston, S. C.
c. 1792-1802

CARY, I. H. & CO.
Boston, Mass.

I.H.CARY&CO.

CARY, LEWIS
  Boston, Mass.
  1798-1834

CASE, GEORGE
  E. Hartford, Conn.
  1779

CASEY, GIDEON
  Providence, R. I.
  S. Kingston, R. I., 1753
  1726-1786

CASEY, SAMUEL
  South Kingston, R. I.
  1723-1773

CASHELL, RANDALL H.
  Philadelphia, Pa.
  1807

CASSEDY, ANDREW
  Philadelphia, Pa.
  1840

CASTAN, STEPHEN & CO.
  (J) (W)
  Philadelphia, Pa.
  1819

  ⌈SC & Co⌉

CASTON, FRANCOIS
  New York, N. Y.
  1804

CERNEAU, JOHN
  New York, N. Y.
  1823

CERNEAU, JOSEPH
  New York, N. Y.
  1807

CERNEAU & CO.
  New York, N. Y.
  1811

CHADWICK, THOMAS
  Philadelphia, Pa.
  1809

  ⌈T.C. & H.⌉

CHALMERS, JAMES, SR.
  Annapolis, Md.
  1749

  ⌈IC⌉

CHALMERS, JOHN
  Annapolis, Md.
  w. 1752-1768

  ⌈IC⌉

CHAMBERLAIN, WILSON
  Portsmouth, N. H.
  1839

CHAMPLIN, JOHN
  New London, Conn.
  1745-1800

  ⌈I·C⌉

CHANDLER, STEPHEN
  New York, N. Y.
  1812

  CHANDLER

CHANDLESS, WILLIAM
  New York, N. Y.
  1846

CHAPIN, AARON
  Hartford, Conn.
  1753-1838

CHAPIN, ALEXANDER
Hartford, Conn.
1838

CHAPIN, S.

| S.CHAPIN |

CHAPMAN, DAVID W.
Rochester, N. Y.
w. 1834-1841

CHARTERS, JAMES
New York, N. Y.
1844

CHARTERS, CANN & DUNN
New York, N. Y.
1850

CHASE, J. D.
New York, N. Y.
1820

CHASE & EASTON
Brooklyn, N. Y.
1837

CHASLEY
Boston, Mass.
1764

CHAT, EASTON
Philadelphia, Pa.
1793

CHAT, LE SIEUR
New York, N. Y.
1790

CHAUDRON'S & RASCH
Philadelphia, Pa.
1812

CHAUDRON, SIMON
Philadelphia, Pa.
1798

CHAUDRON, SIMON, AND CO.
Philadelphia, Pa.
1807

SC&Co

CHEDELL, JOHN H.
Auburn, N. Y.
1806-1875

CHEDELL

CHENE, DANIEL
New York, N. Y.
1786

CHERRY, JAMES
Philadelphia, Pa.
1824

CHEVALIER, CLEMENT E.
Philadelphia, Pa.
1816

CHEVALIER & TANGUY
Philadelphia, Pa.
1816

CHILDS, GEORGE K.
Philadelphia, Pa.
c. 1830

G.K.CHILDS

CHITRY, PETER
New York, N. Y.
w. 1814-25

[P. Chitry]

CHITTENDEN, BERIAH
New Haven, Conn.
1751-1827

CHITTENDEN, EBENEZER
New Haven, Conn.
1726-1812

[EC] [EC] [E.CHITTENDEN]

CHURCH, JOSEPH
Hartford, Conn.
New Haven, Conn.
1794-1876

[J. CHURCH]

CHURCH, RALPH
Buffalo, N. Y.
1832

CHURCH & ROGERS
Hartford, Conn.
1825

[CHURCH & ROGERS]

CHURCHILL & TREADWELL
Boston, Mass.
1805

[CHURCHILL Treadwell]

CHURCHILL, JESSE
Boston, Mass.
1773-1819

[J·CHURCHILL]

[CHURCHILL]

CHURCHWELL, CHARLES
Philadelphia, Pa.
1781

CLAPP & RIKER
New York, N. Y.
1802

CLAPP, A. L.
New York, N. Y.
1802

[A.L.CLAPP]

CLAPP, PHILIP
New York, N. Y.
1802

CLARK & ANTHONY
New York, N. Y.
1790

[CLARK & ANTHONY]

CLARK & BRO.
Norwalk, Conn.
1825

CLARK. &BRO. NORWALK

CLARK & COIT
Norwich, Conn.
1820

CLARK & PELLETREAU (J)
New York, N. Y.
1819

[C&P]

CLARK, ANDREW
New York, N. Y.
1744

CLARK, C. & G.
Boston, Mass.
1833

CLARK, CHARLES
Boston, Mass.
1798

CLARK, CURTIS
New York, N. Y.
1823

CLARK, F. H. & CO.
Memphis, Tenn.
c. 1850

[F.H.CLARK &C°]
[MEMPHIS]

CLARK, GABRIEL D.
Baltimore, Md.
1813-1896

[G.D.CLARK]

CLARK, GEORGE C.
Providence, R. I.
1824

[G.C.CLARK]

CLARK, GEORGE D.
Baltimore, Md.
1826

[G.D.CLARK]

CLARK, HENRY
Philadelphia, Pa.
1813

CLARK, I.
Boston, Mass.
1754

[I·C] [I.CLARK] [I..CLARK]
[I.CLARK] [CLARK]

CLARK, I. & H.
New York, N. Y.
1812

[I.&H·CLARK]

CLARK, J. H.
New York, N. Y.
1815

[J.H.CLARK]

CLARK, JOSEPH
Danbury, Conn.
w. 1791-d. 1821

[JC] [J·CLARK]

CLARK, LEVI
Norwalk, Conn.
1801-1875

[CLARK] [NORWALK]

CLARK, LEWIS W. (J)
Utica, N. Y.
c. 1835

[L.W.CLARK]
[UTICA]

CLARK, METCALF B.
Boston, Mass.
1835

CLARK, PELLETREAU & UPSON
Charleston, S. C.
1823

CLARK, PETER G.
New Haven, Conn.
1810

CLARK, RICHARD
New York, N. Y.
1795

CLARK, SAMUEL
Boston, Mass.
1681

CLARK, THOMAS
Boston, Mass.
1725-1781

CLARK, WILLIAM
New Milford, Conn.
1750-1798

CLARKE, JAMES
Newport, R. I.
1734

CLARKE, JONATHAN
Newport, R. I.
w. 1734-d. 1770

CLEVELAND & POST
Norwich, Conn.
1815

CLEVELAND, AARON
Norwich, Conn.
1820
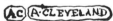

CLEVELAND, BENJAMIN
Newark, N. J.
c. 1800

CLEVELAND, WILLIAM
Norwich, Conn.
Ohio, w. 1808-1830
1770-1837

CLINE, CHARLES
Philadelphia, Pa.
1829

CLUET, JOHN
Kingston, N. Y.
1725

CLUSTER, ISAAC D.
St. Louis, Mo.
1850

COBB, EPHRAIM
Boston, Mass.
1708-1777

COBURN, JOHN
Boston, Mass.
1725-1803

CODDINGTON, JOHN
Newport, R. I.
1690-1743

CODMAN, WILLARD
Boston, Mass.
1839

CODNER, JOHN
Boston, Mass.
1754-1782

Top left: tankard by Benjamin Wynkoop. (*Courtesy The Metropolitan Museum of Art*). Right: tankard by Philip Syng, Jr. (*Courtesy Philadelphia Museum of Art*). Bottom left: tankard by Benjamin Burt. Right: tankard by Cornelius Kierstede. (*Both photos Courtesy of The Metropolitan Museum of Art*).

COE & UPTON
New York, N. Y.
1840

COE L UPTON

COE, L. P.
New York, N. Y.

L.P.COE

COEN, C. E. & CO.
New York, N. Y.
1810

C.COEN & CO

COEN, DANIEL B.
New York, N. Y.
w.c. 1787-1805

DC   D.COEN

COFFMAN, WILLIAM
Philadelphia, Pa.
1839

COGSWELL, HENRY
Boston, Mass.
w.c. 1845-1853

H.COGSWELL

COHEN, BARROW A.
New York, N. Y.
1825

COHEN, THOMAS
Chillicothe, O.
Before 1814

COHEN, WILLIAM
Alexandria, Va.
1833

COIGNARD, LOUIS
New York, N. Y.
1805

COIT & MANSFIELD
Norwich, Conn.
1816-1819

 C&M   C&M

COIT, E.
Norwich, Conn.
w. 1825-*d.* 1839

E.COIT

COIT, THOMAS C.
Norwich, Conn.
1791-1841

T.C.C.

COLE, ALBERT
New York, N. Y.
1844

COLE, EBENEZER
New York, N. Y.
1818

E.COLE

COLE, JACOB
Philadelphia, Pa.
1785

COLE, JOHN
Boston, Mass.
1686

COLEMAN, BENJAMIN
Burlington, N. J.
1795

B.COLEMAN

COLEMAN, C. C.
Burlington, N. J.
1835

COLEMAN, JOHN
New York, N. Y.
1814

COLEMAN, NATHANIEL
Burlington, N. J.
w. from 1790

COLEMAN, S.
Burlington, N. J.
1805

COLEMAN, WILLIAM
Baltimore, Md.
1783

COLES, ALBERT
New York, N. Y.
c. 1840

COLES, JOHN A.
New York, N. Y.
1830

COLEY, SIMEON
New York, N. Y.
1767

COLEY, WILLIAM (J)
New York, N. Y.
w.c. 1766-1804

COLEY, WM. & SIMEON
New York, N. Y.
before 1766

COLLET, J. B.
New York, N. Y.
1805

COLLETTE, LAMBERT
Buffalo, N. Y.
1835

COLLINS AND FORBES
New York, N. Y.
1825

COLLINS, ARNOLD
Newport, R. I.
1690

COLLINS, SELDEN
Utica, N. Y.
w. 1837-1850

COLLINS, W. & L.
New York, N. Y.
1830

COLNER, JOHN
New York, N. Y.
1818

COLONEL, JOHN
Philadelphia, Pa.
1804

COLTON & BALDWIN
New York, N. Y.
1819

COLTON & COLLINS (J)
New York, N. Y.
1832

COLTON, DEMAS JR. (J)
New York, N. Y.
1826

D.COLTON Jᵈ

COLTON, LEVI
New York, N. Y.
1825

COLTON, OREN
New York, N. Y.
1818

COLWELL & LAWRENCE
Albany, N. Y.
1850

CONEY, JOHN
Boston, Mass.
1655-1722

CONLYN, T.
Philadelphia, Pa.
c. 1845

T.CONLYN

CONNELL, M.
Philadelphia, Pa.
1800

M:CONNELL

CONNING, J.
Mobile, Ala.
1840

J.CONNING

CONNOR, JOHN H.
New York, N. Y.
1835

J.H.CONNOR

J.H.CONNOR

CONNOR, JOHN W.
Norwalk, Conn.
1836

CONYERS, JOSEPH
Boston, Mass.
1708

CONYERS, RICHARD
Boston, Mass.
1688

COOK & CO.
New York, N. Y.
1797

COOK, BENJAMIN E.
Northampton, Mass.
w. 1825-1835

B.E.COOK
NORTHAMPTON

COOK, ERASTUS
Rochester, N. Y.
1793-1864

E.COOK

COOK, JOHN
New York, N. Y.
1795

| J.COOK | COOK |
| JCOOK | JCOOK |

COOKE & CO.
Philadelphia, Pa.
1785

COOKE, J. B.

J.B.COOKE

COOKE, JOSEPH
Philadelphia, Pa.
1785

COOLEY, OLIVER B.
Utica, N. Y.
1828

COOLEY

COOLIDGE, JOSEPH
Boston, Mass.
1747-1821

Coolidge   Coolidge

COOPER
Philadelphia, Pa.
1816

COOPER & FISHER
New York, N. Y.
1850

COOPER & YONGUE
Columbia, S. C.
1852

COOPER, B.
New York, N. Y.
1814

COOPER, B. & J.
New York, N. Y.
1810

B&J
COOPER

COOPER, FRANCIS W.
New York, N. Y.
1846

F.W.C.   F.W.COOPER.
N.Y.

COOPER, JOHN
New York, N. Y.
1814

COOPER, JOSEPH
New York, N. Y.
1770

COPP, JOSEPH
New London, Conn.
1732-1815

J.COPP

COPP, NATHANIEL P.
Albany, N. Y.
1834

CORBETT, J.

CORBETT   J.CORBETT

CORLEY, WILLIAM
New York, N. Y.
1811

CORNELISON, CORNELIUS
New York, N. Y.
1712

CORNELIUS, CHRISTIAN
Philadelphia, Pa.
1810

C.CORNELIUS

CORNWELL, N.
Danbury, Conn.
1776-1837

N.CORNWELL

CORNELL, WALTER
Providence, R. I.
1780

CORNELL

CORRIN, JOSIAH
Philadelphia, Pa.
1823

CORTELYOU, JACQUES W.
New Brunswick, N. J.
1781-1822

J.W. CORTELYOU.

COURCELLE, HILAIRE
New Orleans, La.
1822

COUVERTIE, LOUIS
New Orleans, La.
1822

L'COUVERTIE

COVERLY, JOHN
Boston, Mass.
w.c. 1788

I.COVERLY

COVERLY, THOMAS
Newburyport, Mass.
1730-1800

T.COVERLY

COWAN, WILLIAM D.
Philadelphia, Pa.
1808

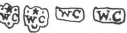

COWELL, WILLIAM
Boston, Mass.
1682-1736

COWELL, WILLIAM, JR.
Boston, Mass.
1713-1761

W.Cowell W.Cowell

COWLES, RALPH
Cleveland, Ohio
c. 1850

COWLES COWLES

COX, J. & I. (John & James)
New York, N. Y.
1817-1853

 J❀ICOX

J.&I.C.

COX, J. & I., & CLARK
New York, N. Y.
c. 1830

J&IC&C

COX, JOHN
Philadelphia, Pa.
1818

CRAFT, STEPHEN
New York, N. Y.
1811

CRAIG, JAMES
Williamsburg, Va.
1750

CRANDALL, BENJAMIN
Providence, R. I.
Portsmouth, N. H.
c. 1830

CRANE, STEPHEN M.
New York, N. Y.
1813

CRANSTON, SAMUEL
Newport, R. I.
1684

CRAWFORD, JOHN
New York, N. Y., 1815-1820
Philadelphia, Pa., 1837

| J CRAWFORD |
| 9 Crawford |

CREW, J. T.
Albany, N. Y.
1849

CRITTENDEN, NEWTON E.
Cleveland, Ohio
1826-1872

| N.E. CRITTENDEN |

CRONE, HENRY
Cleveland, Ohio
1780

CROSBY, JONATHAN
Boston, Mass.
b. 1743, w. 1796

| JC |

CROSBY, SAMUEL T.
Boston, Mass.
1850

CROSS, WILLIAM
Boston, Mass.
b. 1658, w.c. 1700

| WC |

CROUCKESHANKS, A.
Boston, Mass.
1768

CUMMINGS, DAVID B.
Philadelphia, Pa.
1811

CURRAN, I. B.
Ithaca, N. Y.
1835

| I.B.CURRAN |

CURRIER, A. S.

| A.S.Currier |

CURRIER, EDMUND M.
Salem, Mass.
1830

CURRIER & TROTT
Boston, Mass.
1836

Currier & Trott

CURRIN, JOSEPH
Philadelphia, Pa.
1829

CURRY, JOHN
Philadelphia, Pa.
1831

J. CURRY

CURRY & PRESTON
Philadelphia, Pa.
1831

CURRY & PRESTON   C & P

CURTIS, JOEL
Wolcott, Conn.
b. 1786

CURTIS, LEWIS
Farmington, Conn.
b. 1774, w. to 1820

L·CURTIS

CURTIS, THOMAS
New York, N. Y.
1835

CURTISS & CANDEE
Woodbury, Conn.
1825

CURTISS & DUNNING
Woodbury, Conn.
1828

CURTISS & STILES
Woodbury, Conn.
after 1825

CURTISS & STILES

CURTISS, CANDEE & STILES
Woodbury, Conn.
after 1825

CURTISS·CANDEE & STILES

C.C.& S.

CURTISS, DANIEL
Woodbury, Conn.
1801-1878

CUSHMAN, ISAAC
Boston, Mass.
1823

CUTLER, A.
Boston, Mass.
c. 1842

A.CUTLER   BOSTON

CUTLER, EBEN
Boston, Mass.
1846

E.CUTLER

CUTLER, J. N.
Albany, N. Y.
1849

CUTLER, RICHARD
New Haven, Conn.
1736-1810

CUTLER, RICHARD, JR.
New Haven, Conn.
1774-1811

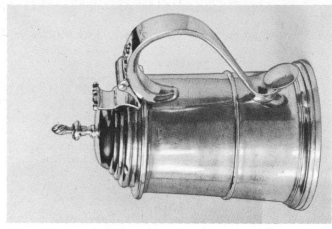

Left: tankard by Edward Winslow. (*Courtesy Philadelphia Museum of Art*). Center: tankard by Henricus Boelen. (*Courtesy The Metropolitan Museum of Art*). Right: tankard by John Hancock. (*Courtesy of The Metropolitan Museum of Art*).

CUTLER, RICHARD & SONS
New Haven, Conn.
c. 1800

CUTLER, SILLIMAN & WARD
New Haven, Conn.
from 1767

CUTLER, WILLIAM
New Haven, Conn.
1785-1817

CUTLER, WILLIAM
Portland, Me.
1823

D

DAGGETT, HENRY
New Haven, Conn.
1741-1830

DALLON, JOHN
Philadelphia, Pa.
1791

DALLY, PHILLIP
New York, N. Y.
1779

PD

DALLY & HALSEY
New York, N. Y.
1787

DANA, PEYTON
Providence, R. I.
1800-1849

P DANA

DANE, THOMAS
Boston, Mass.
1723-1796

T. DANE   T. DANE

DANIEL, PERRY O.
Boston, Mass.
c. 1830

PERRY O. DANIEL

DANIELS, CHARLES W.
Troy, N. Y.
1836

DARBY, JOHN
Charleston, S. C.
w. 1801-1831

DARBY, WILLIAM
Charleston, S. C.
w. 1790-1797

DARBY

DARGEE, JOHN
New York, N. Y.
1810

DARROW, DAVID
New York, N. Y.
1825

DARROW, EDMUND
New York, N. Y.
w. 1843-1861

DARROW

DARROW, JOHN F.
Catskill, N. Y.
1818

DARROW

DAUBAYSON, VICTOIRE
Philadelphia, Pa.
1820

DAUCE, SIMON
Philadelphia, Pa.
1798

DAVENPORT, JONATHAN
Baltimore, Md.
w. 1789-1801
Philadelphia, Pa.
after 1793

DAVENPORT, ROBERT
Philadelphia, Pa.
1808

DAVENPORT, SAMUEL
Milton, Mass.
1741

DAVERNE, JOHN
Baltimore, Md.
1799

DAVID & DUPUY
Philadelphia, Pa.
1792

DAVID, JOHN
Philadelphia, Pa.
1736-1794

DAVID, JOHN JR.
Philadelphia, Pa.
w. 1785-1805

DAVID, LEWIS A.
Philadelphia, Pa.
1823

DAVID, PETER
Philadelphia, Pa.
1691-1755

DAVIS & BABBITT
Providence, R. I.
1820

DAVIS & BROWN
Boston, Mass.
1809-1820

> DAVIS & BROWN

DAVIS & WATSON
Boston, Mass.
1815

> DAVIS WATSON & CO

DAVIS, EDWARD
Newburyport, Mass.
d. 1781

> EDAVIS EDavis
> ED EDavis

DAVIS, ELIAS
Boston, Mass.
w. 1805-1825

> ELIAS DAVIS

DAVIS, JOSHUA G.
Boston, Mass.
1796

DAVIS, PALMER & CO.
Boston, Mass.
1841

Davis, Palmer & Co.

Davis Palmer & Co.

DAVIS, SAMUEL
Boston, Mass.
w. 1801-1842

S. DAVIS   DAVIS

DAVIS, THOMAS A.
Boston, Mass.
w. 1825-1830

T.A.DAVIS

T·A·DAVIS

DAVIS, WILLIAM
Boston, Mass.
1823

DAVIDSON, BRAZILLAI
Norwich, Conn.
1740-1828

DAVIDSON, CHARLES
Norwich, Conn.
1805

DAVISON, CLEMENT (J)
New York, N. Y.
w. 1819-1838

C DAVISON   C.DAVISON

DAVY, ADAM
Philadelphia, Pa.
1795

DAWES, WILLIAM
Boston, Mass.
1766

DAWS, R.
1800

R·DAWS

DAWSON, JOHN
New York, N. Y.
1769

DAWSON, WILLIAM
Philadelphia, Pa.
1763

DAY, JOHN
Boston, Mass.
w. 1820-1825

DEANE, JAMES
New York, N. Y.
1760

DEAS, DAVID
Philadelphia, Pa.
1831

DECKER, JAMES
Troy, N. Y.
c. 1830

J.DECKER

DE FOREST & CO.
New York, N. Y.
1827

D&CO.

DELAGROW, ANDREW
Philadelphia, Pa.
1795

DELANO, JABEZ
New Bedford, Mass.
1763-1848

DE LAROUX, JOHN
New Orleans, La.
1822

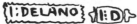

DELAUNEY, JEAN
New York, N. Y.
1805

DEMILT, ANDREW
New York, N. Y.
1805

DEMMOCK, JOHN
Boston, Mass.
1798

DEMORSY, JEAN
New Orleans, La.
1822

DEMORT, JOHN
New York, N. Y.
1810

DEMORT, LUCIEN
New York, N. Y.
1810

DENHAM, D. C.
New York, N. Y.

DC Denham

DENISE, JOHN
New York, N. Y.
1798

DE NISE, JOHN
Philadelphia, Pa.
1698

DENISE, JOHN & TUNIS
New York, N. Y.
1798

DENISON, T.
New York, N. Y.
1790

T. DENISON

DENNIS, EBENEZER
Hartford, Conn.
b. 1753

DENNIS & FITCH
Troy, N. Y.
1836

DENNIS, GEORGE
Norwich, Conn.
b. 1749

DE PARISIEN, OTTO PAUL
New York, N. Y.
from 1764

OP OPDP

DE PARISIEN, OTTO P. & SON
New York, N. Y.
c. 1790

DE PEYSTER, WILLIAM
New York, N. Y.
1733

DE REMIER, CORNELIUS B.
Ithaca, N. Y.
1804

DE REMIER, JACOB R.
New York, N. Y.
c. 1830

DE REMIER & MEAD
Ithaca, N. Y.
c. 1830

DE REMIER, PETER
New York, N. Y.
1738-1814

PDR

DESHON, DANIEL
New London, Conn.
1697-1781

DESQUET & TANGUY
Philadelphia, Pa.
1805

DESURET, LEWIS
Philadelphia, Pa.
1799

DEVERELL, JOHN
Boston, Mass.
1764-1813

Deverell

DEXTER, JOHN
Marlboro, Mass.
1756

DE YOUNG, MICHAEL
Baltimore, Md.
w. 1816-1836

M·DEYOUNG·

DICKERSON, H. & CO.
Philadelphia, Pa.
1815

DICKERSON, JOHN
Morristown, Mass.
1778

DICKINSON & ROBINSON
Philadelphia, Pa.
1796

DICKINSON, JONATHAN
Philadelphia, Pa.
1794

DIKEMAN, AARON (J)
New York, N. Y.
w. 1824-1837

A.DIKEMAN

DIMMOCK, JOHN
New York, N. Y.
1801

DIMOND, ISAAC M.
New York, N. Y.
c. 1830

DISBROW, G. E.
New York, N. Y.
c. 1825

G.E.DISBROW NEW YORK

DIXON, ISAAC (J)
Philadelphia, Pa.
c. 1845

I.DIXON

DIXWELL, BASIL
Boston, Mass.
1732

DIXWELL, JOHN
Boston, Mass.
1680-1725

ID

DOANE, JOSHUA
Providence, R. I.
w. 1740, d. 1753

DOANE   DOANE

I DOANE

DOBBS
New York, N. Y.
1788

DOBLEMAN, FREDERICK
Philadelphia, Pa.
c. 1810

DODGE, BENJAMIN
Boston, Mass.
1836

DODGE, EZEKIEL
New York, N. Y.
1792

E Dodge   E DODGE

DODGE, EZRA
New London, Conn.
1766-1798

DODGE, JOHN
New York, N. Y., 1790
Catskill, N. Y., 1818

J·DODGE

DODGE, NEHEMIAH
Providence, R. I.
w. 1795-1824

N·DODGE

N.DODGE

DODGE, SERIL
Providence, R. I.
1765-1803

S·DODGE

DOLE, DANIEL N.
Portsmouth, N. H., 1805
Newburyport, Mass., 1811

D·N·DOLE

DOLE, E. G.
Portsmouth, N. H.
1820

EG Dole

DOLER, DANIEL
Boston, Mass.
1765

DOLL, J.
New York, N. Y.
c. 1820-1830

J. DOLL

DOLL, W. H.
New York, N. Y.
c. 1845

WHDoll.

W. DOLL

DONALON, JOHN W.
Boston, Mass.
1823

DONOVAN, WILLIAM
Philadelphia, Pa.
1785

W DONOVAN

DONTREMEI, C.
Philadelphia, Pa.
1805

DOOLITTLE, AMOS
New Haven, Conn.
1754-1832

AD AD

DOOLITTLE, ENOS
Hartford, Conn.
1781

DORAN, JOHN
Cincinnati, Ohio
1826

DORGY, PETER
Philadelphia, Pa.
1816

DORRANCE
c. 1800

DORSEY, JOSHUA
Philadelphia, Pa.
1793-1804

I·DORSEY

DORSEY, SAMUEL
Philadelphia, Pa.
1804

DORSEY, SIMON
Philadelphia, Pa.
1820

DORWIG, CHRISTOPHER
Philadelphia, Pa.
1765

DOSTER, MICHAEL
Philadelphia, Pa.
1831

DOUGLAS, ALEXANDER
New York, N. Y.
1792

DOUGLAS, CANTWELL
Baltimore, Md.
1799

DOUGLAS, JAMES W.
Philadelphia, Pa.
1791

J Douglas

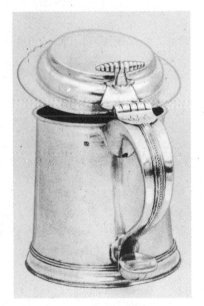

Top left: tankard by Garret Onclebagh. Right: tankard by Nicolas Roosevelt. Bottom left: tankard by Simeon Soumain. Right: tankard by Cornelius Kierstede. (*Courtesy of The Metropolitan Museum of Art*).

DOUGLAS, ROBERT
New London, Conn.
1740-1796

DOUGLASS & HECKMAN
Philadelphia, Pa.
1837

DOUGLASS, JEREMOTT W.
Philadelphia, Pa.
c. 1790

DOUGLASS, JOHN
Philadelphia, Pa.
1840

DOUTIEMER, CULE
Philadelphia, Pa.
1791

DOWIG, GEORGE C.
Philadelphia, Pa.
w. 1765-1791

DOWNES, J.
Philadelphia, Pa.
1770

DOWNING & BALDWIN (J)
New York, N. Y.
c. 1835

DOWNING & PHELPS
New York, N. Y.
1810

DOWNING, G. R.
New York, N. Y.
1810

DRAPER, JOSEPH
Wilmington, Del.
w. 1816-1832

DREWRY, GEORGE
Philadelphia, Pa.
1763

DRINKER, JOHN
New York, N. Y.
1835

DROWN, T. P.
Boston, Mass., 1790
Portsmouth, N. H.
w. 1803-1816

DROWNE, BENJAMIN
Portsmouth, N. H.
1759-1793

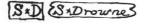

DROWNE, SAMUEL
Portsmouth, N. H.
1749-1815

 ‹S✶Drowne›

DROWNE, SHEM
Boston, Mass.
1749

(S D)

DRUMONT, ANTOINE
New York, N. Y.
1808

DUBOIS & CO.
New York, N. Y.
1803

DUBOIS, ABRAHAM
Philadelphia, Pa.
w. 1777-1807

(AD) A DUBOIS

A·DUBOIS

DUBOIS, A.
New York, N. Y.
1803

DUBOIS, JOSEPH
New York, N. Y.
w. 1790-1797

J·DUBOIS I·DUBOIS

DUBOIS, PHILO
Buffalo, N. Y.
w. 1842-1848

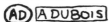

DUBOIS, TUNIS D.
New York, N. Y.
1799

T·D·DUBOIS

T·D·D

DUCHE & DONARD
Philadelphia, Pa.
1820

DUCHE, RENE
New York, N. Y.
1795

DUDLEY, BENJAMIN
Birmingham, Ga.
1768

DUFFEL, JAMES
Georgetown, S. C.
c. 1790-1800
New York, N. Y.
from 1801

I·DUFFEL

DUHME & CO.
Cincinnati, Ohio
1839

DUMMER, JEREMIAH
Boston, Mass.
1645-1718

(ID) (ID)

DU MORTE, JOHN
Philadelphia, Pa.
1796

DUMOURIER, JOSEPH
Philadelphia, Pa.
1816

DUMOUTET, JOHN B.
Philadelphia, Pa.
w. before 1802; after 1813
Charleston, S. Car.
w. 1802-1813

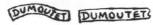

DUNBAR & BANGS
Worcester, Mass.
c. 1850

DUNBAR, R. D.
Worcester, Mass.

DUNDAS, PRATT
Philadelphia, Pa.
1837

DUNKERLY, JOSEPH
Boston, Mass.
1787

DUNLEVY, ROBERT
Philadelphia, Pa.
1831

DUNN & CANN
New York, N. Y.
1837

DUNN, CAREY
New York, N. Y., 1765
Newark, N. J., 1782

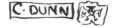

DUNN, DAVID
New York, N. Y.
1835

DUNN & SON
New York, N. Y.
1787-1791

DUNSCOMB, DENNIS
New York, N. Y.
1765

DUON, H.
Baltimore, Md.
1819

DUPUY, BARNARD
Raleigh, N. C.
w. 1833-1840

DUPUY, DANIEL
Philadelphia, Pa.
1719-1807

DUPUY, DANIEL JR.
Philadelphia, Pa.
w. 1772-1812

DUPUY, JOHN
Philadelphia, Pa.
1770

DUPUY, JOHN & DANIEL, JR.
Philadelphia, Pa.
1783

DUPUY & SONS
Philadelphia, Pa.
1784

DURANDEAU, JOHN
New York, N. Y.
1835

DURGIN, WILLIAM B.
Concord, N. H.
1850

> Wm. B. Durgin

> Concord N. H.

DUSENBERRY, W. C.
New York, N. Y.
w. 1819-1835

> W.C. DUSENBERRY

DUTEUS, CHARLES J.
Philadelphia, Pa.
1751

DUTEUS & HARPER
Philadelphia, Pa.
1755

DUVALIER
c. 1800

> DUVALIER

DUYCKINCK, DANIEL
New York, N. Y.
1798

> D.DUYCKINK

DWIGHT, TIMOTHY
Boston, Mass.
1654-1691

E

EAGLES & MORRIS
New York, N. Y.
1799

EAMES, JOSHUA
Boston, Mass.
1828

EASTMAN, SETH
Concord, N. H.
1820

> SETH.EASTMAN

EASTON, JAMES
Nantucket, Mass.
1807-1903

> J.EASTON 2ᵈ

> PURE Coin

> J.EASTON NANTUCKET

EASTON, NATHANIEL
Nantucket, Mass.
1780

> N.EASTON

EASTON & SANFORD
Nantucket, Mass.
1830-1838

> E&S

> EASTON & SANFORD

> Easton & Sanford

EASTWICK, THOMAS
Boston, Mass.
1743

◄{ 73 }►

EATON, JAMES B.
Boston, Mass., *c.* 1805
Charleston, S. C., 1829

EATON, TIMOTHY
Philadelphia, Pa.
1793

EAYRES, THOMAS S.
Boston, Mass.
1760-1803

EDGAR, JOHN
New York, N. Y.
1807

EDMECHAT, CLAUDE
New York, N. Y.
1790

EDMUNDS, B. F.
XIX Century

B.F. EDMUNDS

EDWARDS, ABRAHAM
Ashby, Mass.
1763

EDWARDS, ANDREW
Boston, Mass.
1796

EDWARDS, CALVIN
Ashby, Mass.
1710

EDWARDS, JOHN
Boston, Mass.
1671-1746

EDWARDS, JOSEPH
Boston, Mass.
1707-1777

EDWARDS, JOSEPH, JR.
Boston, Mass.
1737-1783

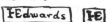

EDWARDS, SAMUEL
Boston, Mass.
1705-1762

EDWARDS, SAMUEL
Natick, Mass.
1726-1783

EDWARDS, THOMAS
Boston, Mass.
1701-1755

EDWARDS, THOMAS
New York, N. Y.
1731

EMBREE
c. 1790

EMBREE

ELDERKIN, ALFRED
> Killingsworth, Conn.
> 1759-1833

ELDERKIN, ELISHA
> New Haven, Conn.
> 1753-1822

ELDERKIN & STANIFORD
> Windom, Conn.
> 1790

ELFRETH, JEREMIAH
> Philadelphia, Pa.
> 1723-1765

ELLIOT, H.
> XIX Century

ELLIOTT, GEORGE
> Wilmington, Del.
> c. 1835

ELLIOTT, JAMES
> Winnsboro, S. C.
> 1807

ELLIOTT, JOHN A.
> Sharon, Conn.
> b. 1788; w. 1857

ELLIOTT, JOSEPH
> New Castle, Del.
> 1768

ELLIS, LEWIS W.
> Philadelphia, Pa.
> 1837

ELLISTON, PETER
> New York, N. Y.
> w. 1791-1800

ELLSWORTH, DAVID
> Windsor, Conn.
> 1742-1821

ELTONHEAD, THOMAS
> Baltimore, Md.
> 1835

EMERY, STEPHEN
> Boston, Mass.
> 1752-1801

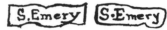

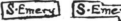

EMERY, THOMAS K.
> Boston, Mass.
> 1781-1815

EMERY & CO.
> New York, N. Y.
> 1798

EMMONS, L.

ENGLAND, GEORGE
> New York, N. Y.
> c. 1800

ENGLAND, WILLIAM
Philadelphia, Pa.
1717

ENSIGN
c. 1800

ENSIGN

EOFF & CONNOR
New York, N. Y.
1833

J.H.CONNOR & GEOFF

EOFF & HOWELL
New York, N. Y.
1805

EOFF & HOWELL

EOFF & MOORE
New York, N. Y.
1835

G.EOFF & J.C.MOORE

EOFF & PHYFE
New York, N. Y.
1844

E&P

EOFF & SHEPARD
New York, N. Y.
1825

E&S

EOFF, EDGAR M.
New York, N. Y.
c. 1850

EME

EOFF, GARRET
New York, N. Y.
1779-1858

G.EOFF G.Eoff

EOLLES & DAY
Hartford, Conn.
1825

EOLLES & DAY
HARTFORD

EPPS, ELLERY
Boston, Mass.
1808

EQUER & AQUIMAC
New York, N. Y.
1816

ERWIN, ANDREW
Philadelphia, Pa.
1837

ERWIN, HENRY
Philadelphia, Pa.
w. 1817-1829

H.ERWIN H.ERWIN

ERWIN, JAMES
Baltimore, Md., 1809
New York, N. Y., 1815

J.ERWIN

ETTER, B.
c. 1780

B.ETTER

ETTING, BENJAMIN
New York, N. Y.
1769

EVANS, HENRY
New York, N. Y.
1820

EVANS, JOHN
New York, N. Y.
1830

|EVANS|

EVANS, ROBERT
Boston, Mass.
1768-1812

RE R·E R.EVANS
EVANS EVANS

EVERITT, JESSE
New York, N. Y.
1811

EVERSTEN, JOHN
Albany, N. Y.
1813

EWAN, JOHN
Charleston, S. C.
w. 1823-1852

J.EWAN J.EWAN

EWAN, WILLIAM H.
Charleston, S. C.
w. 1849-1859

WᴴH.EWAN

EYLAND, JAMES
Charleston, S. C.
w. 1819-1835

J.EYLAND

EYLAND, JAMES, & CO.
Charleston, S. C.
w. 1820-1827

F

FABER, WILLIAM
Philadelphia, Pa.
1837

FABER & HOOVER
Philadelphia, Pa.
1837

FAGALER, GEORGE M.
Philadelphia, Pa.
1808

FAIRCHILD, JAMES L.
New York, N. Y.
1830

FAIRCHILD, JOSEPH
New Haven, Conn.
1824

J FAIRCHILD

FAIRCHILD, ROBERT
Durham, Conn.
New Haven, Conn., from 1772
1703-1794

RF RF R·FAIRCHILD
R+F R.FAIRCHILD

FAIRMAN, GIDEON
New London, Conn.
1774-1827

FALES, I.
XIX Century

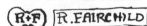

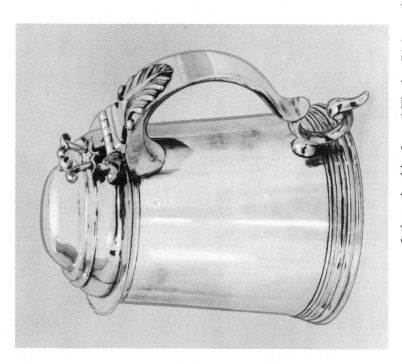

Left: tankard by Samuel Tingley. Right: tankard by Garret Onclebagh, engraved with the Shelley coat of arms. (*Both photos Courtesy of The Metropolitan Museum of Art*).

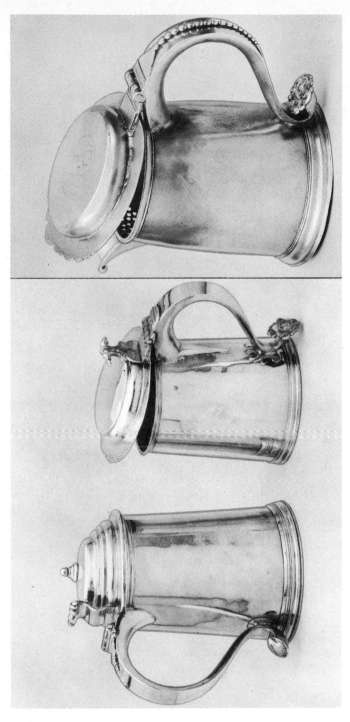

Left: two tankards of the colonial period by Jonathan Clarke and Thomas Savage. Right: tankard attributed to Benjamin Wynkoop. (*Both photos Courtesy of The Metropolitan Museum of Art*).

FARIS, CHARLES
Boston, Mass.
1790

Cˢ Faris   Chaˢ Faris

Chas Faris

FARIS, WILLIAM (W)
Annapolis, Md.
1728-1804

W·F   WF   W.F.

FARLEY, CHARLES
Portland, Me.
1812

FARLEY

C.FARLEY

FARNAM, HENRY
Boston, Mass.
1799

H.FARNAM

FARNAM, R. & H.
Boston, Mass.
1807

R.&H;FARNAM

FARNAM, RUFUS
Boston, Mass.
w. 1796-1833

R.FARNAM

FARNAM, THOMAS
Boston, Mass.
c. 1830

Th:Farnam

FARNAM & WARD
Boston, Mass.
1816

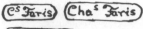
FARNAM & WARD

FARNHAM & OWEN
1810

FARR, JOHN C.
Philadelphia, Pa.
w. 1824-1840

J.C:FARR

JOHN C FARR

FARRINGTON & HUNNEWELL
Boston, Mass.
c. 1840-1850

FARRINGTON & HUNNEWELL

F&H

FARRINGTON, JOHN
Boston, Mass.
1826

FAULKNER, JOHN W.
New York, N. Y.
1835

J.W.FAULKNER   371 Pearl St.

J.W.F.

FECKHART, AUGUST
Rochester, N. Y.
c. 1850

FELLOWS & GREEN
Maine
1825

FELLOWS & GREEN

FELLOWS & STORM
Albany, N. Y.
1839

FELLOWS & STORM

FELLOWS, ABRAHAM
Newport, R. I.
c. 1820

FELLOWS

FELLOWS, J. K.
Lowell, Mass.
c. 1830

J.K.FELLOWS

FELLOWS, I. W. & J. K.
Lowell, Mass.
1834

I.W. & J.K. FELLOWS

FELLOWS, JOHN F.
Portsmouth, N. H.
1824

FELT, J. S.
Portland, Me.
1825

J.S.FELT

FENNO, J.
1825

J.Fenno

FENNO & HALE
Bangor, Me.
1840

FENNO & HALE

FERGUSON, JOHN
Philadelphia, Pa.
1802

FERRIER, JOHN
New Orleans
1802

FERRIS, BENJAMIN
New York, N. Y.
1816

FERRIS, R.
c. 1850

R.FERRIS

FERRIS, ZIBA
Wilmington, Del.
w. 1810-1860

ZIBA FERRIS

FESSENDEN
Newport, R. I.
1845

FESSENDEN   PURE SILVER

FEURT, PETER
New York, N. Y.
1703-1737

FIELD, PETER (W)
New York, N. Y.
w. 1808-1837

P.FIELD JR

FIELDING, GEORGE
New York, N. Y.
1731

FIELDS, SAMUEL
Philadelphia, Pa.
1816

FIFIELD, JOHN S.
Westerly, R. I.

FINCH, HIRAM
Albany, N. Y.
1840

FINEWELL, SAMUEL
New York, N. Y.
1835

FINLAYSON
Charleston, S. Car.
1782

FIRENG, J. P.
Burlington, N. J.
1810

| J.P.FIRENG | BURLINGTON N.J. |

FISHER, JAMES
New York, N. Y.
1821

FISHER, THOMAS
Philadelphia, Pa.
1797

| T.Fisher | T.FISHER |
| T Fisher | |

FITCH, ALLEN
New Haven, Conn.
b. 1785

FITCH, DENNIS M.
Troy, N. Y.
1840

| D.M.FITCH |

FITCH & HOBART
New Haven, Conn.
1811-1813

FITCH, JOHN
Trenton, N. J.
1743-1798

| J.FITCH | ✿ | ✿ |

FITE, JOHN (W)
Baltimore, Md.
1810

| I·FITE |

FLAGG, JOSIAH
Boston, Mass.
1765

| J.F |

FLAGG, JOSIAH, JR.
Boston, Mass.
1810

FLAGG, S.
c. 1825

| S·FLAGG· |

FLERE & HARRIS
Philadelphia, Pa.
1767

FLETCHER & BENNETT
Philadelphia, Pa.
1837

FLETCHER & GARDINER
Philadelphia, Pa.
1812-1825

| F&G |

FLETCHER, CHARLES
>Philadelphia, Pa.
>1817

FLETCHER, THOMAS (J)
>Philadelphia, Pa.
>w. 1814-1850

T.F.

T.FLETCHER
PHILAD.

FLING, GEORGE
>Philadelphia, Pa.
>1749

FLOTT, LEWIS
>Baltimore, Md.
>1817

FOLLOPPE, A. A.
>Boston, Mass.
>1808

FOLSOM, JOHN
>Albany, N. Y.
>1781

FOOTE, WILLIAM
>East Haddam, Conn.
>b. 1772

FORBES, ABRAHAM G.
>New York, N. Y.
>1769

AGF   AF N.YORK

FORBES, BENJAMIN G.
>New York, N. Y.
>1817

FORBES, C. & J. W.
>New York, N. Y.
>c. 1820

C.& I.W. FORBES

T   ✳

FORBES, COLIN V. G.
>New York, N. Y.
>1816

CVGF

C. FORBES   U

FORBES, C. V. G. & SON
>New York, N. Y.
>1835

FORBES & SON

FORBES, GARRET
>New York, N. Y.
>w. 1808-1837

G. FORBES

FORBES, JOHN W.
>New York, N. Y.
>w. 1802-1835

I WF   I WF   I.W.FORBES
NY   N.Y   I W FORBES

FORBES, WILLIAM
>New York, N. Y.
>1830

W.FORBES

WF   ✳   NEW YORK

W. FORBES   N.Y.   N. YORK

FORBES, WILLIAM G.
New York, N. Y.
w. 1773-1809

W.G FORBES

W.G. FORBES   N·YORK

WG Forbes   WG Forbes

FORCE, JABEZ W.
New York, N. Y.
1819

J.W. FORCE

FORD, SAMUEL
Philadelphia, Pa.
1797

SF

FOREST, ALEXANDER
Baltimore, Md.
1802

FORMAN, BENONI B.
Albany, N. Y.
1813

FORREST, ALEXANDER
Baltimore, Md.
1802

FORTUNE, ANTHONY
Philadelphia, Pa.
1767

FOSTER, ABRAHAM
Philadelphia, Pa.
1816

FOSTER, GEORGE B.
Salem, Mass.
w. 1838-1854

GEORGE B. FOSTER

FOSTER, I.
1761

FOSTER, JOHN
Boston, Mass.
from 1795

FOSTER, JOHN
New York, N. Y.
1811

J.FOSTER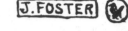

FOSTER, JOSEPH
Boston, Mass.
1760-1839

I·FOSTER

FOSTER

FOSTER, N. & T.
Newburyport, Mass.
w. 1823-1860

N.&T. FOSTER

FOSTER & RICHARDS
New York, N. Y.
1815

J.F   T. RICHARDS

FOSTER, SAMUEL
Boston, Mass.
1676-1702

FOSTER, THOMAS
Newburyport, Mass.
1823

T·FOSTER

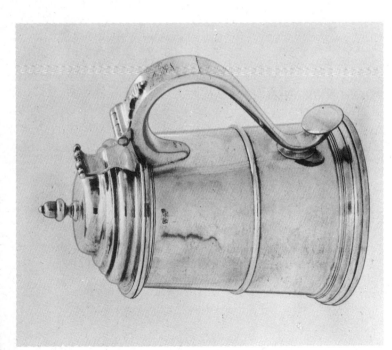

Left: tankard by Benjamin Burt. Right: tankard by Bartholomew Schaats. (*Both photos Courtesy of The Metropolitan Museum of Art*).

FOURNIQUET, LOUIS
New York, N. Y.
w. 1795-1823

FOURNIQUET & WHEATLEY
New York, N. Y.
1817

FOWLER, GILBERT
New York, N. Y.
1825

FRADGLEY, THOMAS
New York, N. Y.
1797

FRANCIS, E.
c. 1820

[E.FRANCIS]

FRANCIS, JULIUS C.
Middletown, Conn.
1785-1862

FRANCIS, NATHANIEL
New York, N. Y.
w. 1804-1819

[N·FRANCIS] [FRANCIS]
[N·FRANCIS] [MM]

FRANCISCUS, GEORGE
Baltimore, Md.
1776

[G·FRANCISCUS]

FRANCISCUS, GEORGE, JR.
Baltimore, Md.
to 1818

FRANK, JACOB
Philadelphia, Pa.
1793

FRANKS, WILLIAM
Philadelphia, Pa.
1839

FRASER, WILLIAM
Philadelphia, Pa.
1735

FREEBORN, N.
c. 1800

[N·FREEBORN]

FREEMAN & WALLIN
Philadelphia, Pa.
1850

[FREEMAN & WALLIN]
[☆] [♤] [♡] [☆]

FREEMAN, WILLIAM
Philadelphia, Pa.
1839

FREEMANS, J. M. & CO.
c. 1800

[J.M.FREEMANS & CO]

FRIES, J.

FRINTH, JAMES
Philadelphia, Pa.
1840

FROBISHER, BENJ. C.
Boston, Mass.
1792-1862

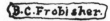

FROST & MUMFORD
Providence, R. I.
1810

FROTHERINGHAM, EBENEZER
Boston, Mass.
1756-1814

FRYER, JOHN W.
Albany, N. Y.
1784

FUETER, DANIEL C.
New York, N. Y.
w. 1754-1770

FUETER, DAVID
New York, N. Y.
1789

FUETER, LEWIS
New York, N. Y.
1775

FULLER, ALEXANDER
New York, N. Y.
1811

FURIS, LEWIS
New York, N. Y.
1810

FURSDON, ROGER
Charleston, S. C.
1784

G

GADLEY & JOHNSON
Albany, N. Y.
1849

GAFKINS, J.
Providence, R. I.
1832

GAITHER, GREENBURY
Washington, D. C.
1834

GALE & HAYDEN
New York, N. Y.
1846

GALE & MOSELY
New York, N. Y.
1830

GALE & STICKLER
New York, N. Y.
1823

GALE & WILLIS
New York, N. Y.
1840

GALE&WILLIS

GALE, JOHN
New York, N. Y.
c. 1820

J.GALE   J.GALE

GALE, J. L.
New York, N. Y.
1819

J.L.G.   J.L.GALE

GALE, WILLIAM
New York, N. Y.
1816

W.G   [P]   [S]

GALE, WILLIAM, JR.
New York, N. Y.
1799-1867

WM.GALE JR.

GALE, WILLIAM, & SON
New York, N. Y.
w. 1823-1850

W.G&S   [◇]

GALE, WOOD & HUGHES
New York, N. Y.
1835-1845

G.W&H

GALLUP, CHRISTOPHER
Ledyard, Conn.
1764-1849

GALT, SAMUEL
Williamsburg, Va.
1749

GARDINER, B.
New York, N. Y.
1829

GARDINER, BALDWIN (J)
Philadelphia, Pa.
w. 1814-1838

B·G   B.GARDINER
B·G&CO

GARDINER, B. & CO.
New York, N. Y.
1836

B.GARDINER&CO
BG&CO

GARDINER, JOHN J.
Boston, Mass.
1730-1776

GARDINER, SIDNEY
Philadelphia, Pa.
1810

GARDNER, BENJ. F.
Mass.-R. I.
w. 1817

GARDNER, JOHN
New London, Conn.
1734-1776

JG   JG   J.GARDNER

GARLAND, WILLIAM

W.GARLAND   [☆]   [D]   [◙]

GARNER, JOHN
Cincinnati, Ohio
1825

GARRE, S.
New York, N. Y.
1825

[S G] [SGARRE]

GERREN, ANTHONY
Philadelphia, Pa.
1813

GARRETSON, ELIAKIM
Wilmington, Del.
1785

[E. GARRETSON]

GARRETT, PHILIP (J)
Philadelphia, Pa.
w. 1801-1835

[P GARRETT]

GARRETT, THOMAS C.
Philadelphia, Pa.
c. 1830-1840

[T.C. GARRETT]

GARRETT, T. C. & CO.
Philadelphia, Pa.
c. 1830

[T.C.GARRETT & CO]

GARRISON, JOHN
New York, N. Y.
1825

GARROCH. A.

[A GARROCH]

GARROW & DORSEY
Baltimore, Md.
c. 1800

GASKINS, J.
Norfolk, Va.
c. 1830

[J Gaskins]

GASKINS, W. W.
Norfolk, Va.
1806

[WWG]

GATHAM, WILLIAM
Philadelphia, Pa.
1802

GAULTIER, FRANCIS
Charleston, S. C.
1759

GAY, CHARLES
Baltimore, Md.
1779

GAY, NATHANIEL
Boston, Mass.
1664

GAZLAY, S.

[S GAZLAY]

GEDDES, JAMES
Williamsburg, Va.
c. 1760

GEE, JOSEPH
Philadelphia, Pa.
1785

[GEE]

GEFFROY, NICHOLAS
Newport, R. I.
1761-1839

[N.GEFFROY.]   [GEFFROY]

[N.GEFFROY]

GIESSENDAUER, JOHN U.
Charleston, S. C.
1737

GELEY, PETER
Philadelphia, Pa.
1793

GELSTON & CO.
New York, N. Y.
1837

[GELSTON&CO]

GELSTON & GOULD
Baltimore, Md.
1819

GELSTON & TREADWELL
New York, N. Y.
1836

GELSTON, GEORGE S.
New York, N. Y.
1833

[G.S.GELSTON]

GELSTON, HUGH
Baltimore, Md.
1794-1873

[HU.GELSTON]

[GELSTON]

GELSTON, LADD & CO.
New York, N. Y.
1836

[GELSTON LADD & CO]

GELSTON, WELLES
Boston, Mass.
c. 1815

[Welles Gelston]

W. T. & T. V. GENDAR
c. 1850

[W.T. & T.V. GENDAR]

GEORGEON, BERNARD
Philadelphia, Pa.
1797

GERMON, JOHN D.
Philadelphia, Pa.
w. 1782-1825

[I G]

[GERMON] [PHILA]

GERRISH, A.
c. 1800-1810

[A GERRISH]

GERRISH & PEARSON
New York, N. Y.
c. 1800

[Gerrish & Pearson]

GERRISH, TIMOTHY
Portsmouth, N. H.
1753-1813

[T G] [T. Gerrish]

[GERRISH] [T Gerrish]

1790 1770 1810 1760

1760 1770 1760

1780 1710 1800 1810

1820 1820 1820

GETHEN, JOHN W.
Philadelphia, Pa.
1811

IWG 🐢 🐚

GETHEN, WILLIAM
Philadelphia, Pa.
1797

W.GETHEN

GETTY, JAMES
Williamsburg, Va.
1772

GETZ, PETER
Lancaster, Pa.
1792

P.Getz

GHISELIN, CESAR
Philadelphia, Pa.
1670-1734

CG   CG

CG

GHISELIN, WILLIAM
Philadelphia, Pa.
w. 1751-1762

WG   GHISELIN

GIBBS, DANIEL
Boston, Mass.
1716

GIBBS, JOHN
Providence, R. I.
d. 1797

J GIBBS

GIBBS, JOHN F.
Providence, R. I.
1803

GIBNEY, MICHAEL
New York, N. Y.
w. 1836-1845

GIBSON, WILLIAM
Philadelphia, Pa.
1845

GIBSON

GIFFING, CHRISTOPHER
New York, N. Y.
w. 1815-1835

C.Gifing.N.Y

GIFFORD, E.
Fall River, Mass.
1825

E.GIFFORD
FALL RIVER

GILBERT, SAMUEL
Hebron, Conn.
c. 1798

SG   SG

GILBERT, WILLIAM W.
New York, N. Y.
w. 1767-d. 1818

WG   N.YORK   GILBERT
W.Gilbert   Gilbert   N.York

GILBERT & CUNNINGHAM
New York, N. Y.
1839

GILL, CALEB
Boston, Mass.
1774-1855

GILL

GILL, LEAVITT
Hingham, Mass.
1810

GILLEY, PETER
Philadelphia, Pa.
1797

GILMAN, BENJ. C.
Exeter, N. H.
1763-1835

BCG

GILMAN, JOHN W.
New York, N. Y.
1771-1823

I·W·G

GINOCHIO, JOHN B.
New York, N. Y.
1837

J.B.GINOCHIO

GIQUEL, JOHN B. F.
New Orleans, La.
1822

GIRARD, FRANCIS
Philadelphia, Pa.
1817

GIRAUD, HENRY
New York, N. Y.
1805

GIRREAUN, STEPHEN
Philadelphia, Pa.
1785

GIVEN, A.
Albany, N. Y.
1849

GLAZE & RADCLIFFE
Columbia, S. C.
1848-1851

GLIDDEN, JOSEPH
Boston, Mass.
1707-1780

GODDARD, D. & SON
Worcester, Mass.
1845

D.GODDARD & SON

D. GODDARD & Co.

GOELET, PHILIP
New York, N. Y.
w. 1731-1747

PG PG PG

GOFORTH, JEREMIAH
Philadelphia, Pa.
1700

GOLDTHWAITE, JOSEPH
Boston, Mass.
1706-1780

I·G I·G I·G

GOMBACH, JOHN
Philadelphia, Pa.
1802

GOODHUE, D. T.
Boston, Mass.
1840

GOODHUE, JOHN
Salem, Mass.
w. 1822-1855

J.GOODHUE

GOODING, HENRY (W)
Boston, Mass.
1833

GOODING GOODING

GOODING, JOSEPH
Boston, Mass.
1815

GOODING, JOSIAH
Boston, Mass.
w. 1841-1859

Josiah Gooding

GOODWIN, ALLYN
Hartford, Conn.
1797-1869

GOODWIN, BENJAMIN
Boston, Mass.
1812

B:Goodwin

GOODWIN & DODD
Hartford, Conn.
1812

G&D

GOODWIN, H. & A.
Hartford, Conn.
1811

GOODWIN

GOODWIN, HORACE
Hartford, Conn.
1787-1864

GOODWIN, RALPH
Hartford, Conn.
1828

GORDON, A. & J.
New York, N. Y.
1798

GORDON, ALEXANDER
New York, N. Y.
1795

GORDON

GORDON, ANDREW
New York, N. Y.
1796

GORDON & CO.
Boston, Mass.
1849

GORDON, GEORGE
Newburgh, N. Y.
w. 1800-1824

G.Gordon

GORDON, JAMES
New York, N. Y.
1795

GORDON, JAMES S.
Philadelphia, Pa.
1769

GORHAM & THURBER
Providence, R. I.
1850

Gorham&Thurber

GORHAM & WEBSTER
New York, N. Y.
1831

Gorham & Webster

GORHAM, WEBSTER & PRICE
Providence, R. I.
1835

GORHAM WEBSTER & PRICE

GORHAM, JABEZ
Providence, R. I.
from 1815

J GORHAM

GORHAM, JABEZ & SON
Providence, R. I.
1842

J.GORHAM&SON

GORHAM, JOHN
New Haven, Conn.
1814

GORHAM, MILES
New Haven, Conn.
1757-1847

M.G   M.GORHAM

GORHAM, RICHARD
New Haven, Conn.
1775-1841

GOUGH, JAMES
New York, N. Y.
w. 1769-1795

JG

GOULD, J.
Baltimore, Md.
1795-1874

GOULD, JAMES
Baltimore, Md.
1816-1868

J·GOULD   J.GOULD
10-15

GOULD, JOHN
Philadelphia, Pa.
1840

GOULD, STOWELL & WARD
Baltimore, Md.
1840

GOULD & WARD
Baltimore, Md.
1850

OULD &WARD

GOVERT, JAMES
Philadelphia, Pa.
1802

GOWDEY, JOHN & WM.
Charleston, S. C.
w. 1757-c. 1795

GOWEN, WILLIAM
Medford, Mass.
1772

WG   W·GOWEN

◄{ 95 }►

GRAHAM, DANIEL
West Sheffield, Conn.
1789

GRANT, THOMAS
Marblehead, Mass.
1754
[T·GRANT]

GRANT, WILLIAM
Philadelphia, Pa.
w. 1785-1814

GRAVELLE, RENE S.
Philadelphia, Pa.
1813

GRAVES, THOMAS
Cincinnati, Ohio
1828

GRAVIER, NICHOLAS
New Orleans, La.
1822

GRAY, G.
Portsmouth, N. H.
1839
[G·GRAY]

GRAY, JOHN
New London, Conn.
1692-1720
[I.G] [IG]

GRAY, ROBERT
Portsmouth, N. H.
d. 1850
[R·Gray] [ROBT·GRAY]
[ROBT GRAY]

GRAY, SAMUEL
New London, Conn.
1684-1713
[GRAY]

GRAY, SAMUEL
Boston, Mass.
1732
[S: GRAY]

GREEN, JAMES
New York, N. Y.
1805

GREENBURY, GAITHER
Washington, D. C.
c. 1820

GREEN, BENJAMIN
Boston, Mass.
1712-1776
[B:GREEN]

GREENE, RUFUS
Boston, Mass.
1707-1777
[R·G] [R·G] [R·G] [R·G]
[R·GREENE] [R·GREENE]
[R.GREENE]

GREENE, WM. & CO.
Providence, R. I.
1815

GREENLEAF, DAVID
Norwich, Conn.
1737-1800
[D. Greenleaf]

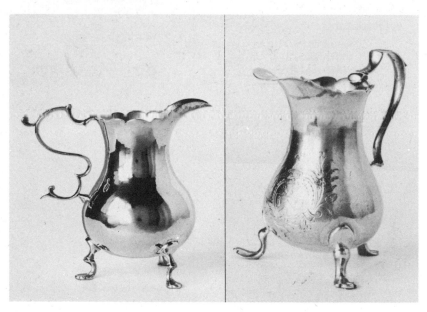

Top left: creamer by William Ghiselin. (*Courtesy Philadelphia Museum of Art*). Right: creamer by Benjamin Burt. Bottom left: creamer by Samuel Casey. Right: creamer by Benjamin Burt. (*Courtesy of The Metropolitan Museum of Art*).

GREENLEAF, DAVID, JR.
Hartford, Conn.
1765-1835

GREENLEAF

GREENLEAF, JOSEPH
New London, Conn.
1779-1798

GREFFIN, PETER
Philadelphia, Pa.
1801

GREGG & HAYDEN
Charleston, S. C.
w. 1843-1846

GREGG, HAYDEN & CO.
(Retailers)
New York, N. Y.
Charleston, S. C.
w. 1846-1852

GREGG HAYDEN & CO

GREGG, WILLIAM
Columbia, S. C.
c. 1830

GRIFFEN & HOYT (W)
Albany, N. Y.
1830

GRIFFEN & HOYT

GRIFFEN & HOYT ✦✦✦

GRIFFEN, PETER (W)
Albany, N. Y.
1825

PGRIFFEN

GRIFFEN & SON (W)
Albany, N. Y.
1832

GRIFFEN & SON

GRIFFETH, DAVID
Portsmouth, N. H.
1768

GRIFFING, CHRISTOPHER
New York, N. Y.
1816

CGriffing NY

GRIGG, WM.
New York, N. Y.
w. 1765-1795

Grigg · Grigg

Grigg · W. GRIGG

GRIGNON, BENJAMIN
Boston, Mass.
1685

GRIGNON, RENE
Norwich, Conn.
w. 1708-1715

GRIMKE, JOHN P.
Charleston, S. C.
1744

GRISCOM, GEORGE
Philadelphia, Pa.
1791

GRISELM, CAESAR
Philadelphia, Pa.
1700

GRISWOLD, GILBERT
Middletown, Conn.
1825

GRISWOLD, WILLIAM
Middletown, Conn.
1820

W.GRISWOLD

GROEN, JACOB M.
New York, N. Y.
w. 1701-*d.* 1750

IM

GUERCY, DOMINICK
New York, N. Y.
1795

GUERIN, ANTHONY
Philadelphia, Pa.
1791

GUEST, HENRY B.
Philadelphia, Pa.
1778

GUILLE, NOAH
Boston, Mass.
1701

GUINAND, FRED'K E. (J)(W)
Baltimore, Md.
1814

GUINAND

GUIRNA, ANTHONY
Philadelphia, Pa.
1796

GUNN, ENOS
Waterbury, Conn.
b. 1770

ENOS GUNN
E.GUNN

GURLEY, WILLIAM
Norwich, Conn.
b. 1764, *w.* 1804

W.G

GURNEE, BENJAMIN
New York, N. Y.
1820

GURNEE

GURNEE, B. & S.
New York, N. Y.
1833

GURNEE & CO.
New York, N. Y.
1820

GUTHRE, JAMES
Wilmington, Del.
1796-1877

J. GUTHRE

GUTHRE & JEFFERIS
Wilmington, Del.
1840

H

HACKLE, WILLIAM
Baltimore, Md.
1776

HADDOCK & ANDREWS
Boston, Mass.
1838

HADDOCK, HENRY
Boston, Mass.
1836

HADDOCK, LINCOLN & FOSS
Boston, Mass.
1850

HADWEN, WILLIAM
Nantucket, Mass.
1791-1862, *w.* to 1829

W·HADWEN

HADWEN ★

HAGAR, ELIAS
Rochester, N. Y.
w. 1841-1844

HAGGAN, WOLFGUNG
Reading, Pa.
1752

HAGGENMACHER, J. H. & CO.
Philadelphia, Pa.
1836

HAIGHT, NELSON
Newburgh, N. Y.
w. 1839-1852

N.HAIGHT

HAINES, ABRAHAM
New York, N. Y.
1801

HALE, J. R.
J.R. HALE

HALL & BLISS
c. 1780

HALL & BLISS

HALL & BROWER
Albany, N. Y.
1830

HALL & ELTON
Geneva, N. Y.
1841

HALL & HEWSON
Albany, N. Y.
1828-1847

H&H

HALL, HEWSON & BROWER
Albany, N. Y.
c. 1850

HALL, HEWSON & MERRIFIELD
Albany, N. Y.
1814

HALL & MERRIMAN
Albany, N. Y.
New Haven, Conn.
1825

H&M

H&M

HALL, ABIJAH
Albany, N. Y.
1813

HALL, ABRAHAM B.
Geneva, N. Y.
w. 1806-1839

HALL, BROWER & CO.
Albany, N. Y.
1836

HALL, CHARLES
Lancaster, Pa.
w. 1765-1779

CH

HALL, DAVID
Philadelphia, Pa.
w. 1765-1779

DH DHALL

HALL, DREW
New York, N. Y.
1789

HALL, GREEN
Albany, N. Y.
1813

HALL, IVORY
Concord, N. H.
1781

HALL, JOSEPH
Albany, N. Y.
1781

I HALL

HALLAM, JOHN
New London, Conn.
1752-1800

HALSEY, JABEZ
New York, N. Y.
1762-1820

I·HALSEY

I·HALSEY

HALSTED, BENJAMIN
New York, N. Y.
w. 1764-1806

HALSTED·NY

Halsted

HALSTED & SON
New York, N. Y.
1799

HALSTRICK, J.
Boston, Mass.
1846

HAM, GEORGE
Portsmouth, N. H.
1810

HAMILL & CO.
New York, N. Y.
1817

HAMILL, JAMES
New York, N. Y.
1816

J·HAMILL·N.Y.

HAMILTON, JAMES
Annapolis, Md.
1766

HAMILTON, JOHN
New York, N. Y.
1798

HAMLIN, CYRUS
Portland, Me.
1831

HAMLIN, WILLIAM
Middletown, Conn.
Providence, R. I.
1772-1869

W·H WH

HAMLIN

HAMMERSLEY, THOMAS
New York, N. Y.
1727-1781

TH T·H TH

HANCOCK, JOHN
Charlestown, Mass.
Providence, R. I.
1732-1772

J·HANCOCK J·HANCOCK

J·HANCOCK

HANDLE, JOHN
Philadelphia, Pa.
1839

HANFORD, A.
c. 1820-1830

A·HANFORD

HANKS, BENJAMIN
Windham, Conn.
1738-1810
Ashford, Conn.
from 1790

HANNAH, W. W.
Albany, N. Y.
c. 1840

W.W.HANNAH

HANNERS, GEORGE
Boston, Mass.
1697-1740

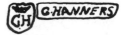

HANNERS, GEORGE, JR.
Boston, Mass.
1721-1760

G·H G.H

HANSELL, J.
Valley Forge, Pa.
1825

HANSELL, ROBERT
Boston, Mass.
1823

HARACHE, PIERRE
Williamsburg, Va.
1691

HARDING, N., & CO.
Boston, Mass.
w. c. 1800-1850

HARDING, NEWELL
Boston, Mass.
1796-1862

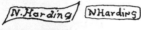

HARDWOOD, JOHN
Philadelphia, Pa.
1816

HARDY, STEPHEN
Portsmouth, N. H.
1781-1843

HARLAND, THOMAS
Norwich, Conn.
1735-1807

HARLAND, THOMAS JR.
Norwich, Conn.
1781-1806

HARPEL, THOMAS W.
Philadelphia, Pa.
1813

HARPER, ALEXANDER
Philadelphia, Pa.

HARPER, DAVID
Philadelphia, Pa.

HARPER, THOMAS W.
Philadelphia, Pa.
1813

HARRIS, CHARLES
Charleston, S. C.
w. 1768-1779

HARRIS, GEORGE
New York, N. Y.
1802

HARRIS, H.
Albany, N. Y.
1820

HARRIS & STANWOOD
Boston, Mass.
1835

HARRIS & WILCOX
Albany, N. Y., 1844
Troy, N. Y.
1847-1850

HART & BLISS
Middletown, Conn.
w. 1803-1804

HART & BREWER
Middletown, Conn.
w. 1800-1803

HART, ELIPHAZ
Norwich, Conn.
1789-1866

HART, JOHN
Philadelphia, Pa.
1776

HART, JOHN J.
New York, N. Y.
1820

HART, JUDAH
Middletown, Conn.
1777-1824

J.HART   J.Hart
JHART

HART & SMITH
Baltimore, Md.
1816

HART&SMITH
H&S

HART & WILCOX
Norwich, Conn.
w. 1805-1807

H&W

HART, WILLIAM
Philadelphia, Pa.
1818

W.HART.

HARTFORD, GEORGE
Philadelphia, Pa.
1794

HARTLEY, SAMUEL
Philadelphia, Pa.
1818

HARTMAN, PHILIP
Philadelphia, Pa.
1813

HARVEY, LEWIS
Philadelphia, Pa.
1811

HARVEY.LEWIS

HASCY, ALEXANDER
Albany, N. Y.
w. 1835-1850

HASCY

HASCY, NELSON
Albany, N. Y.
1849

HASELTON & CO.

HASELTON&CO

HASELTON, IRA
Portsmouth, N. H.
c. 1825

HASKELL, BARNABUS
Boston, Mass.
1833

HASKELL, V. W.

V.W. HASKELL

HASTIER, JOHN
New York, N. Y.
w. 1726, d. c. 1791

IH   IH   IH   IH   J.H

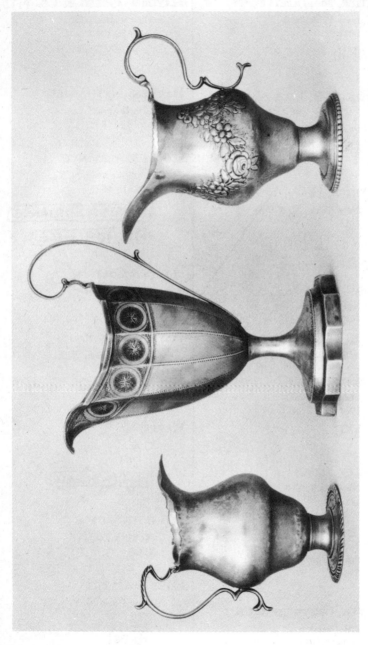

Creamer (*center*) by C. Wiltberger. Others are unidentified. (*Courtesy Philadelphia Museum of Art*).

HASTIER, MARQUETTE
New York, N. Y.
1771

MH

HASTINGS, B. B.
Cleveland, Ohio
w. 1835-1846

HASTINGS

HASTINGS, H.
New York, N. Y. (?)
1815

H.HASTINGS

HAUGH, SAMUEL
Boston, Mass.
1675-1717

SH

HAVERSTICK, WM.
Philadelphia, Pa.
1781

WH

HAWLEY, NOAH
New York, N. Y.
1816

HAWS, JOHN
Philadelphia, Pa.
1837

HAYDEN BROTHERS & CO.
Charleston, S. C.
w. 1852-1855

HAYDEN, GREGG & CO. (J)
Charleston, S. C.
w. 1838-1842

HAYDEN & GREGG

HAYDEN, NATHANIEL
Charleston, S. C.
w. 1832-1843

HAYES & ADRIANCE
Poughkeepsie, N. Y.
w. 1816-1825

HAYES & ADRIANCE

H & ADRIANCE

HAYES & COLTON
Newark, N. J.
1831

HAYES, PETER P.
Poughkeepsie, N. Y.
1835

P.P. HAYES

HAYES, W.
Conn.
c. 1780

WH   W.Hayes

HAYS, ANDREW
Newark, N. J.
1769

HAYS & MYERS
New York, N. Y.
1770

H&M

HEAD, JOSEPH
Philadelphia, Pa.
1798

HEALD, J. S.
Baltimore, Md.
1810

[J·S·HEALD] [IP]

HEALY
Boston, Mass.
1773

HEATH, JOHN
New York, N. Y.
1761

[J·H] [I·HEATH]

[JH]

HEATH, RALPH
Cambridge, O.
w. 1807

HEBBERD
New York, N. Y.
1847

HECK, LEWIS
Lancaster, Pa.
c. 1760

[LH]

HECTOR, JOHN
Charleston, S. C.
1774

HEDGER, GEORGE
Buffalo, N. Y.
w. 1828-1848

HEDGES, DANIEL
Easthampton, N. Y.
1779-1856

[HEDGES]

HELME, NATHANIEL
South Kingston, R. I.
1761-1789

[HELME] [HELME]
[NW]

HEMPSTED, DANIEL B.
New London, Conn.
1784-1852

HEMPSTED & CHADLER
New York, N. Y.
1811

HENCHMAN, DANIEL
Boston, Mass.
1730-1775

[DH] [Henchman]

HENDERSON, A. A.
Philadelphia, Pa.
1837

[A·HENDERSON]
[A·Henderson]

[HENDERSON]

HENDERSON, ADAM
Poughkeepsie, N. Y.
c. 1835

HENDRICKS, AHASUERUS
New York, N. Y.
1676

[AH] [AH]

HENRY, FELIX
New York, N. Y.
1815

HEQUEMBOURG, CHARLES
New Haven, Conn.
c. 1820-1840

HERBERT, TIMOTHY B.
New York, N. Y.
1816

HERILS, FRANCIS
Philadelphia, Pa.
1804

HERON, ISAAC
New York, N. Y.
1768

HEURTIN, WILLIAM
New York, N. Y.
w. 1831, d. c. 1765

HEWS, ABRAHAM
Boston, Mass.
1823

HEWSON, JOHN D.
Albany, N. Y.
1815

HEYDORN & IMLAY
Hartford, Conn.
1810

HEYER & GALE
New York, N. Y.
1807

HEYER, WILLIAM B.
New York, N. Y.
w. 1798-1827

HIGBIE & CROSBY
Boston, Mass.
1820

HILDEBUR
Philadelphia, Pa.
1790

HILL, JAMES
Boston, Mass.
1770

HILL, WILLIAM F. (W)
Boston, Mass.
1810

HILL & WADILL
Petersburg, Va.
1780

HILLDRUP, THOMAS
Hartford, Conn.
w. 1774, d. 1804

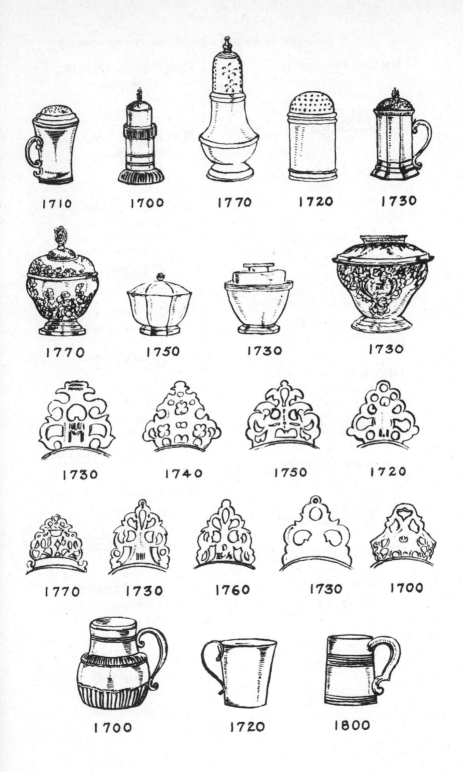

1710   1700   1770   1720   1730

1770   1750   1730   1730

1730   1740   1750   1720

1770   1730   1760   1730   1700

1700   1720   1800

HILLER, BENJAMIN
Boston, Mass.
1687-1745

HILLER, JOSEPH
Boston, Mass.
1745

HILTON, WILLIAM
Philadelphia, Pa.
1814

HIND, JOHN
Philadelphia, Pa.
1760

HINDMAN, D. B. & CO.
Philadelphia, Pa.
w. 1833-1837

HINSDALE & ATKIN (J)
New York, N. Y.
c. 1830

HINSDALE, HORACE (J)
New York, N. Y.
w. 1815-1842

HINSDALE, EPAPHRAS
New York, N. Y.
1797

HITCHBORN, DANIEL
Boston, Mass.
1773

HITCHBORN, SAMUEL
Boston, Mass.
1752

HITCHCOCK, ELIAKIM
Cheshire, Conn.
1726-1788
New Haven, Conn.

HOBART, JOSHUA
New Haven, Conn.
1811

HOBBS, NATHAN
Boston, Mass.
1792-1868

HODGE, JOHN
Hadley, Mass.
c. 1800

HOFFMAN, FREDERICK
Philadelphia, Pa.
1819

HOFFMAN, JAMES M.
Philadelphia, Pa.
1820

HOLLAND, LITTLETON
Baltimore, Md.
1770-1847

HOLLINGSHEAD, JOHN
Philadelphia, Pa.
1768

HOLLINGSHEAD, WM.
Philadelphia, Pa.
w. 1757-1785

HOLLISTER, JULIUS
Oswego, N. Y.
c. 1850

HOLLOWAY, ROBERT
Baltimore, Md.
1822

HOLMES, ADRIAN B. (J)
New York, N. Y.
1801

HOLMES, ISRAEL
Waterbury, Conn.
1768-1802

HOLMES, J.
New York, N. Y.
1816

HOLMES, WILLIAM
New York, N. Y.
1801

HOLSEY, E.
Philadelphia, Pa.
1820

HOLTON, DAVID
Baltimore, Md.
1804

HOLTON, JOHN
Philadelphia, Pa.
1794

HOLYOKE, EDWARD
Boston, Mass.
1817

HOMES, WILLIAM
Boston, Mass.
1717-1782

HOMES, WILLIAM, JR.
Boston, Mass.
1742-1825

HOOD & TOBEY
Albany, N. Y.
1849

HOOKEY, WILLIAM
Newport, R. I.
1750

HOOVER, HENRY
Philadelphia, Pa.
1816

HOOVER, JOSEPH E.
Philadelphia, Pa.
1837

HOPKINS, JESSE
Waterbury, Conn.
b. 1766

HOPKINS, JOSEPH W.
Waterbury, Conn.
1730-1801

HOPKINS, STEPHEN
Waterbury, Conn.
1721-1796

HOPPER, SAMUEL
Philadelphia, Pa.
1835

HORN, E. B.
Boston, Mass.
1847

HOSFORD, HARLEY
New York, N. Y.
1820

HOTCHKISS, DAVID
Syracuse, N. Y.
w. 1847-1855

HOTCHKISS, HEZEKIAH
New Haven, Conn.
w. 1754, d. 1761

HOUGH, SAMUEL
Boston, Mass.
1675-1717

HOULTON & BROWNE
Baltimore, Md.
1799

HOULTON, JOHN
Philadelphia, Pa.
1797

HOULTON, OTTO & FALK
Philadelphia, Pa.
1797

HOUSE, A.

HOUTZELL, JACOB
Philadelphia, Pa.
1801

HOW, DAVID
Boston, Mass.
1790

HOWARD, ABRAHAM
Salem, Mass.
1810

HOWARD, JOHN
Philadelphia, Pa.
1819

[Howard]

HOWARD, N.

[N.HOWARD]

HOWARD, THOMAS
Philadelphia, Pa.
1620

HOWARD, WILLIAM
Boston, Mass.
1800

HOWE, GEORGE C. (W)
New York, N. Y.
1825

[GEORGE C.HOWE]

HOWE, GEORGE C. & CO. (W)
New York, N. Y.
1837

[GEO.C. HOWE & CO.]

HOWE, OTIS
Boston, Mass.
1788

HOWE & GUION (W)
New York, N. Y.
w.c. 1840

[HOWE & GUION]

HOWELL & ARNOLD
Albany, N. Y.
1797

HOWELL, B. H.
Newburgh, N. Y.
w. 1835-1848
Buffalo, N. Y.

[HOWELL]

HOWELL, JAMES
Philadelphia, Pa.
w. 1802-1813

[JHowell] [Howell]
[JHowell]

HOWELL, PAUL
New York, N. Y.
1812

[P.HOWELL]

HOWELL, SILAS W.
Albany, N. Y.
1798

[SWHowell] [SWHowell]

HOYT, GEORGE B.
Albany, N. Y.
c. 1830-1850

[GEO.B.HOYT]

HOYT, HENRY E.
New York, N. Y.
1820

[HENRY HOYT]

HOYT, SEYMOUR (J) (W)
New York, N. Y.
w. 1817-1850

[S.HOYT. PEARL ST]

[S.HOYT]

HUBBAL
Washington, D. C.
1834

HUGHES & BLISS
Middletown, Conn.
from 1806

HUGHES, CHRISTOPHER
Baltimore, Md.
1744-1824

[CH] [C·H]

HUGHES, EDMUND
Middletown, Conn.
1804

[E.HUGHES]

HUGHES & FRANCIS
Middletown, Conn.
w. 1807-1809

HUGHES & HALL

[ES][HUGHES & HALL][✳]

HUGHES, HENRY
Baltimore, Md.
1781

HUGHES, JEREMIAH
Annapolis, Md.
1805

[J.HUGHES]

[JHUGHES] [STERLING]

HUGHES, WILLIAM
Baltimore, Md.
w. 1785-1791

[W.H]

HULBEART, PHILIP
Philadelphia, Pa.
w. 1761, d. 1764

[PH] [P.H]

HULL, JOHN
Boston, Mass.
1624-1683

HULL & SANDERSON
Boston, Mass.
w. 1651-1683

HUMBERT, AUGUSTUS
New York, N. Y.
1818

HUMPHREYS, RICHARD
Philadelphia, Pa.
1772

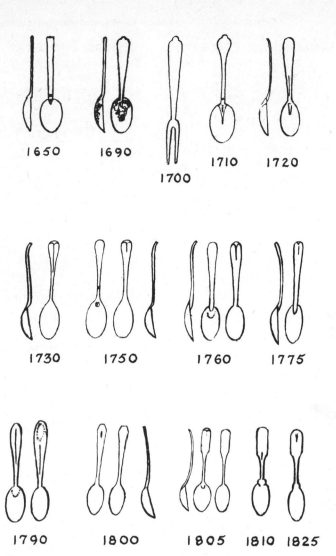

1650   1690   1710   1720

1700

1730   1750   1760   1775

1790   1800   1805   1810 1825

1790

1740

1780

HUMPHREYS, T. B. & SON

HUMPHREYS, THOMAS
Philadelphia, Pa.
1814

HUNLOCK, BOUMAN
Philadelphia, Pa.
1752

HUNNEWELL, GEORGE W.
Boston, Mass.
1836

HUNT, EDWARD
Philadelphia, Pa.
1717

HUNT, WILLIAM
Boston, Mass.
1819

HUNTINGTON, PHILIP
Norwich, Conn.
1770-1825

HUNTINGTON, RICHARD
Utica, N. Y.
w. 1823-1850

HUNTINGTON, ROSWELL
Norwich, Conn.
b. 1763, *w.* 1784

HUNTINGTON, S.
Maine
c. 1850

SHUNTINGTON

HURD, BENJAMIN
Boston, Mass.
1739-1781

HURD, JACOB
Boston, Mass.
1702-1758

HURD, NATHANIEL
Boston, Mass.
1730-1777

HURST, HENRY
Boston, Mass.
1665-1717

HH H·H

HURTIN & BURGI
Bound Brook, N. J.
1766

HUSBAND, JOHN
Philadelphia, Pa.
1796

HUSSEY, STEPHEN
Maryland
1818

S HUSSEY

HUSTON, JAMES
Baltimore, Md.
1799

HUTCHINS, JACOB
New York, N. Y.
1774

HUTCHINS, NICHOLAS
Baltimore, Md.
1777-1845

HUTCHINSON, SAMUEL (W)
Philadelphia, Pa.
1828-1839

HUTTON, GEORGE
Albany, N. Y.
1799

HUTTON, I. & G.
Albany, N. Y.
1799

HUTTON, ISAAC
Albany, N. Y.
1767-1855

HUTTON, JOHN S.
New York, N. Y.
1720

HUYLER, GEORGE (W)
New York, N. Y.
1819
|HUYLER|

HYDE
Newport, R. I.
1730
|HYDE|

HYDE & GOODRICH
New Orleans, La.
1830
|HYDE & GOODRICH|

HYDE & NEVINS
New York, N. Y.
1798-1819
|Hyde & Nevins|

HYMAN, HENRY (W)
Lexington, Ky.
c. 1800
|H. HYMAN R.H.D.|

I

INCH, JOHN
Annapolis, Md.
1721-1763

INGRAHAM, JOSEPH
Portland, Me.
1785

INMAN, BENJAMIN
Philadelphia, Pa.
1816

ISAACS, MICHAEL
New York, N. Y.
1765

IVERS, B.
c. 1800

B·IVERS

J

JACCARD & CO.
St. Louis, Mo.
c. 1850

JACCARD&CO StLOUIS

JACKS, JAMES
Charleston, S. C.
1795

JACKS, WILLIAM
Philadelphia, Pa.
1798

JACKSON, A.
Norwalk, Conn.
1840

A JACKSON

JACKSON, DANIEL
New York, N. Y.
1782

DJ DJACKSON

JACKSON, JAMES
Baltimore, Md.
1775

JACKSON, JOHN
New York, N. Y.
1731

JACKSON

JACKSON, JOSEPH
Baltimore, Md.
1803

JACOB, GEORGE
Baltimore, Md.
1802

G·JACOB

JACOB, MOSES
Philadelphia, Pa.
1775

JACOBS, ABEL
Philadelphia, Pa.
1816

A JACOBS

JACOBS, A., & CO.
Philadelphia, Pa.
1820

A·J & Co

JANVIER, LOUIS
Charleston, S. Car.
1744

JARVIS, MUNSON
Stamford, Conn.
1742-1825, *w.* to 1783

MJ MJ

JAVAIN, HENRY J.
Charleston, S. C.
w. 1835-1838

⟨JAVAIN⟩

JEFFERIS, EMMOR
Wilmington, Del.
1804-1892

[E.JEFFERIS]

JEFFERSON, EPHRAIM
Smyrna, Del.
1788-1844

[E.JEFFERSON]

JENCKES, JOHN C.
Providence, R. I.
1777-1852

J.JENCKES
[JC.JENCKES]

JENCKES & CO.
Providence, R. I.
1798

JENKINS, I. & H.
Albany, N. Y.
1815

[I.&H.Jenkins]

JENKINS, JOHN
Philadelphia, Pa.
1777

[I.J]

JENNINGS, JACOB
Norwalk, Conn.
w.c. 1763-1800

[I.J]

JENNINGS, JACOB, JR.
New London, Conn.
b. 1779, *w.* 1800

JENNINGS & LANDER (W)
New York, N. Y.
1848

JENNINGS & LANDER

JESSE, DAVID
Boston, Mass.
1670-1705

JOHANNES, JOHN M.
Baltimore, Md.
1835

JOHNSON & BALL
Baltimore, Md.
1785

JOHNSON, CHAUNCEY
Albany, N. Y.
w. 1825-1841

[C.JOHNSON]

JOHNSON & GODLEY
Albany, N. Y.
1847

JOHNSON, JOHN
Pittsburgh, Pa.
1815

JOHNSON, MAYCOCK W.
Albany, N. Y.
1815

[M.W.JOHNSON]

JOHNSON & REAT
Baltimore, Md.
1810

JOHNSON & RILEY
Baltimore, Md.
1786

JOHNSON, SAMUEL
New York, N. Y.
w. 1780-1796

JOHNSTON, A.
Philadelphia, Pa.
1830

JOHONNOT, WM. B.
Middletown, Conn.
1766-1849
Windsor, Vt.
from 1792

JONES, A.

JONES, BALL & CO.
Boston, Mass.
1850

JONES, BALL & POOR
Boston, Mass.
1840

JONES, ELISHA
New York, N. Y.
1827

JONES, GEORGE B.
Boston, Mass.
1839

JONES & HUTTON
Wilmington, Del.
1840

JONES, JAMES
Philadelphia, Pa.
1815

JONES, JOHN
Boston, Mass.
1810

JONES, JOHN B.
Boston, Mass.
1782-1854

JONES, JOHN B. & CO.
Boston, Mass.
1838

JONES, LOWS & BALL
Boston, Mass.
1839

[JONES, LOWS & BALL]

JONES, PHILIP
Wilmington, Del.
1843

[P. JONES]

JONES & PEIRCE

[JONES & PEIRCE]

JONES, THOMAS L.

[THOS L. JONES]

[▨] [▨] [D]

JONES & WARD
Boston, Mass.
1815

[JONES & WARD]

JONES, WILLIAM
Marblehead, Mass.
1694-1730

[WI] [WI]

JONES, WILLIAM E.
Rochester, N. Y.
c. 1850

JORDAN, PETER
Philadelphia, Pa.
1823

JOUBERT, P.
Philadelphia, Pa.
1807

JUDAH
New York, N. Y.
1774

JUDSON, HIRAM
Syracuse, N. Y.
w. 1824-1847

H. JUDSON

K

KAY, AMOS
Boston, Mass.
1725

[AK]

KEDZIE, JOHN
Rochester, N. Y.
1809-1889

[J. KEDZIE & CO]

[J KEDZIE] [▨] [▨] [▨]

KEDZIE, J. & CO. (J)
Rochester, N. Y.
1847

KEELER, JOSEPH
Norwalk, Conn.
1786-1824

[JK] [JK] [KEELER]

[KEELER]

KEELER, THADDEUS
New York, N. Y.
w. 1805-1813

[T KEELER]

KEIFF, JOSEPH
Philadelphia, Pa.
1831

KEITH, T. & W.
New York, N. Y.
1805
T.&W.KEITH

KELEY, GRAEL
Boston, Mass.
1823

KELLER, THADDEUS
New York, N. Y.
c. 1800

KELLEY, ALLEN
Providence, R. I.
1810
Nantucket, Mass.
after c. 1825

KELLEY, E. G. & J. S. (W)
Nantucket, Mass.
from 1842
E.&J.Kelley

KELLEY, HENRY A.
Nantucket, Mass.
1815-1869
H.A.Kelley

KELLEY, H. A. & E. G. (W) (R)
Nantucket, Mass.
until 1842
H.A.&E.G.Kelley.

KELLEY, JAMES S. (W)
Nantucket, Mass.
1838-1856
New Bedford, Mass.
after 1856
J.S.Kelley

KENDALL, CHARLES
New York, N. Y.
w. 1780-c. 1805
C.KENDALL

KENDALL, JAMES
Wilmington, Del.
w. 1785-1802
J.KENDALL

KENDALL, S.
S.KENDALL

KENDRICK, AHASUER'S
New York, N. Y.
1698

KENDRICK, WILLIAM
Louisville, Ky.
after 1840
W.KENDRICK.Louisville.

KENNEDY, MATTHEW
Philadelphia, Pa.
1825

KENRICK, ANWYL
Maryland
1775

KEPLINGER, SAMUEL
Baltimore, Md.
1770-1849

KETCHAM, JAMES
New York, N. Y.
w. 1807-1823
Utica, N. Y.
1847

IKETCHAM

KETTELL, THOMAS
Charlestown, Mass.
1760-1850

T.K

KEYWORTH, ROBERT
Washington, D. C.
1831

R.KEYWORTH

KIDNEY, CANN & JOHNSON
New York, N. Y.
c. 1850

K.C.~J.

KIDNEY & DUNN
New York, N. Y.
1844

K&D K&D

KIERSTEDE, CORNELIUS
New York, N. Y.
1674-1757
New Haven, Conn.
from 1725

KIMBALL, LEWIS A.
Buffalo, N. Y.
w. 1837-1842

L.KIMBALL

KIMBERLY, WILLIAM
New York, N. Y.
1792

WK Kimberly KIMBERLY

KING, JOSEPH
Middletown, Conn.
from about 1770

KING, R.

R.KING

KING, THOMAS R.
Baltimore, Md.
1819

TRKING

KINGSTON, JOHN
New York, N. Y.
1775

KINNEY, THOMAS
Norwich, Conn.
1785-1824

TK TK

KINSEY, DAVID (R.)
Cincinnati, Ohio
c. 1830-1850

DAVID KINSEY

DKINSEY

KINSEY, E. & D.
Cincinnati, Ohio
1845

E.&D.KINSEY

KIP, BENJAMIN
New York, N. Y.
1702

KIP, JESSE
New York, N. Y.
1660-1722

$\boxed{\text{IK}}$

KIPPEN, GEORGE
Bridgeport, Conn.
b. 1790, *w.* 1824

$\boxed{\text{G·KIPPEN}}$

KIRBY, WILLIAM
New York, N. Y.
1783

KIRK, SAMUEL
Baltimore, Md.
1793-1872

Service etc. plat.

KIRK & SMITH
Baltimore, Md.
1815-1821

KIRK&SMITH   K&S

KIRKWOOD, PETER
Chestertown, Md.
1790
Annapolis, Md.
c. 1800

$\boxed{\text{PK}}$

KIRTLAND, JOSEPH P.
Middletown, Conn.
b. 1770, *w.* 1796

KITCHEN, ANDREW
Philadelphia, Pa.
1835

KITTS, JOHN
Louisville, Ky.
c. 1840

$\boxed{\text{J.KITTS}}$

KLINE, BARTHOLOMEW
Philadelphia, Pa.
1837

KLINE, B. & CO.
Philadelphia, Pa.
1837

KNAPP, J.

KNEELAND, JOSEPH
Boston, Mass.
1698-1760

$\boxed{\text{I·Kneeland}}$

KRAUSE, JOHN S.
Bethlehem, Pa.
1805

KRIDER & BIDDLE
Philadelphia, Pa.
1850

KRIDER, PETER L.
Philadelphia, Pa.
1850

$\boxed{\text{P.L.K}}$

Left to right: spoon, early 18th century; tablespoon by Paul Revere; funeral spoon by Nicholas Van Rensselaer, inscribed to his wife. (*Courtesy of The Metropolitan Museum of Art*).

Sucket forks by John de Nise. (*Courtesy Philadelphia Museum of Art*).

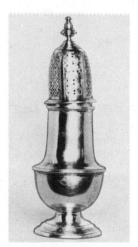

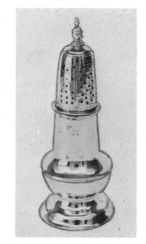

Left to right: caster by John Burt; caster by Nathaniel Helme; caster by Stephen Emery. (*Courtesy of The Metropolitan Museum of Art*).

KUCHER, JACOB
Philadelphia, Pa.
w. 1806-1831

J·KUCHER

KUCHLER, O.
New Orleans, La.
c. 1850

O.KUCHLER
NEW ORLEANS

KUMBEL, WILLIAM
New York, N. Y.
1780

L

LACHAISE, PETER
New York, N. Y.
1794

LADD, WILLIAM F.
New York, N. Y.
1830

WᴹF.LADD   NEW·YORK

LADOMUS, JACOB (J)
Philadelphia, Pa.
w. 1843-1850

J.LADOMUS

LAFAR, JOHN J.
Charleston, S. C.
w. 1806-1849

LAFAR

LAFAR, PETER X.
Charleston, S. C.
w. 1805-1814

LA FORME, ANTOINE
Boston, Mass.
1836

LA FORME, F. J.
Boston, Mass.
1835

LA FORME, VINCENT
Boston, Mass.
1850

V.LAFORME

LA FORME, VINCENT & BRO.
Boston, Mass.
w. 1850-1855

V.L.& Bᴿᴼ   PURE COIN

V.L.&B
PURE COIN

LAINECOURT, STEPHEN
New York, N. Y.
1800

LAKEMAN, E. K.
New York, N. Y.
1799-1857

E.K.LAKEMAN

LAMAR, BENJAMIN (also
Lemar, Lamaire)
Philadelphia, Pa.
w. 1785-1804

BL LAMAR BL

LAMAR, MATHIAS
Philadelphia, Pa.
w. 1781-1796

ML

LAMESIERE, PETER
Philadelphia, Pa.
1811

LAMOTHE, JOHN
New Orleans, La.
1822

LAMPE, JOHN
Baltimore, Md.
1787

LAMSON, J.
c. 1790

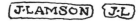

LANDER

LANDER

LANE, AARON
Elizabeth, N. J.
1780

AL

LANG, EDWARD
Salem, Mass.
1742-1830

EL   LANG

LANG, JEFFREY
Salem, Mass.
1708-1758

I·LANG LANG

I·LANG

LANG, NATHANIEL
Salem, Mass.
1736-1826

N·LANG

LANG, RICHARD
Salem, Mass.
1733-1810

R.LANG

LANGE, WILLIAM
New York, N. Y.
1844

·LANGE·

LANGER, JOSEPH
Philadelphia, Pa.
1811

LANSING, JACOB G.
Albany, N. Y.
1736-1803

IGL

LAPEROUSE, JOHN B.
New Orleans, La.
1832

LAROUSSE, PETER
New York, N. Y.
1797

LASHING, PETER
New York, N. Y.
1805

LATHROP, RUFUS
Norwich, Conn.
1731-1805

LATRUIT, JOHN P.
Washington, D. C.
1833

LAWRENCE, MARTIN M. (J)
New York, N. Y.
w. 1832-1840

M.M.LAWRENCE

LAWRENCE, JOSIAH H.
Philadelphia, Pa.
1817

LAWRIE, ROBERT O.
Philadelphia, Pa.
1840

LEA, SAMUEL J.
Baltimore, Md.
w. 1814-1822

LEACH, CHARLES
Boston, Mass.
1765-1814

LEACH, JOHN
Boston, Mass.
1780

LEACH, NATHANIEL
Boston, Mass.
1789

N·L

LEACH, SAMUEL
Philadelphia, Pa.
1745-1780

S·L

LEACH & BRADLEY
Philadelphia, Pa.
1832

LEACOCK, JOHN
Philadelphia, Pa.
w. 1748-1759

LAYCOCK, PETER
Philadelphia, Pa.
1750

LEBLANC, LEWIS
Philadelphia, Pa.
1815

LEDELL, JOSEPH
Philadelphia, Pa.
1797

LE DORC
Philadelphia, Pa.
1797

LEE, SAMUEL W.
Rochester, N. Y.
1785-1861

LEE, SAM'L W., JR.
Rochester, N. Y.
c. 1850

LEFEVRE, F.
Philadelphia, Pa.
1818

LEFEVRE & GRAVELLE
Philadelphia, Pa.
1811

LEFEVRE, JOHN F.
Philadelphia, Pa.
1806

LEGARE, DANIEL
Boston, Mass.
1688-1724

LEGARE, FRANCIS
Boston, Mass.
1657

LE HURAY, NICHOLAS (J)
Philadelphia, Pa.
w. 1809-1831

N.LE HURAY

LE HURAY, NICHOLAS, JR. (J)
Philadelphia, Pa.
w. 1821-1846

N LE HURAY JR

LENDIGREE, M.
New York, N. Y.
1814

LENHART, G.
Bowling Green, Ky.
c. 1840

G Lenhart

LENT, JOHN
New York, N. Y.
1787

J Lent

LENTZ, G. K.

G·K·LENTZ

LEONARD, ALLEN
New York, N. Y.
1830

A.LEONARD

LEONARD, J.

J:LEONARD.

LEONARD, SAMUEL T.
Baltimore, Md.
1786-1848

LEONARD

S.LEONARD

LEONARD & WILSON
Philadelphia, Pa.
1847

L&W   STANDARD

LERET, PETER
Baltimore, Md.
w. 1787-1802

PL   PL eret

LE ROUX, BARTHOLOMEW
New York, N. Y.
w. 1687-*c.* 1710

LE ROUX, BARTHOLOMEW II
New York, N. Y.
1717-1763

BR   BR   BR

LE ROUX, CHARLES
New York, N. Y.
1689-1745

CR

LE ROUX, JOHN
New York, N. Y.
c. 1723

LEWIS, J. H.
Albany, N. Y.
c. 1810

LESCURE, EDWARD
Philadelphia, Pa.
w. 1822-1850

LETELIER, JOHN
Philadelphia, Pa.
w. 1770-1784

LETOURNEAUX
New York, N. Y.
1797

LEVELY
Baltimore, Md.
1788

LEVERETT, KNIGHT
Boston, Mass.
1703-1753

LEVY, JONAS (J)
New York, N. Y.
c. 1835

LEWIS, HARVEY
Philadelphia, Pa.
w. 1811-1826

LEWIS, ISAAC
Huntington, Conn.
1773-1860
Ridgefield, Conn.
w. 1809

LEWIS & SMITH
Philadelphia, Pa.
1805-1811

LEWIS, TUNIS
New York, N. Y.
1805

LEWYN, GABRIEL
Baltimore, Md.
1771

LIBBY, J. G. L.
Boston, Mass.
1820-1846

LIDDEN, JOHN
St. Louis, Mo.
1850

LIGHTFOOT, JAMES
New York, N. Y.
1749

Top: teapot by R. and W. Wilson. Bottom: tea set by Fletcher and Gardiner. (*Courtesy of Philadelphia Museum of Art*).

LINCH, PETER
New York, N. Y.
1805

LINCOLN, A. L.
St. Louis, Mo.
1850

[A.L.Lincoln]

LINCOLN, ELIJAH
Boston, Mass.
1794-1861

[E.Lincoln]

LINCOLN & FOSS
Boston, Mass.
c. 1850

[LINCOLN & FOSS]

LINCOLN & GREEN
Boston, Mass.
1810

[L & G]

LINCOLN & READ
Boston, Mass.
w. 1835-1844

[LINCOLN & READ]

LINDNER, GEORGE
Philadelphia, Pa.
1837

LINDSLEY, CLARK
Hartford, Conn.
w. 1843

[C.LINDSLEY]

LINGLEY, HENRY
New York, N. Y.
1810

LINK, PETER
Philadelphia, Pa.
1811

LINTOT
New York, N. Y.
1762

LITTLE, PAUL
Portland, Me.
1760

[P.L]

LITTLE, WILLIAM
Newburyport, Mass.
1775

[W.L] [WL]

LOCKWARD,

[ᴵᴵ.LOCKWARD]

LOCKWOOD, ALFRED (J)
New York, N. Y.
w. 1817-1837

[A.LOCKWOOD]

[ALFRED LOCKWOOD]
[N.YORK]

LOCKWOOD, FREDERICK
New York, N. Y.
w. 1828-1845

[F.LOCKWOOD]

LOCKWOOD, JAMES
New York, N. Y.
1799

[J.LOCKWOOD]

LOFLAND, PURNEL
Philadelphia, Pa.
1810

LOGAN, ADAM
New York, N. Y.
1803

A·LOGAN

LOGAN, JAMES
Philadelphia, Pa.
1810

LOMBARD, B. E.
Charleston, S. Car.
c. 1830

LOMBARD

LONG, ANDREW
Philadelphia, Pa.
1837

LONG, N.

N·LONG

LONG, WILLIAM
Philadelphia, Pa.
1807

LONGLEY & DODGE
Charleston, S. Car.
c. 1810

LONGLEY, HENRY
New York, N. Y.
1810

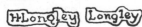 H·Longley Longley

LOOMIS, G. & CO.
Erie, Pa.
1850

G·LOOMIS&CO ERIE

LORD, BENJAMIN
Pittsfield, Mass.
w. 1786-1796

B·LORD

LORD, JABEZ C.
New York, N. Y.
w. 1823-1835

J·LORD

LORD, JOSEPH
Philadelphia, Pa.
1815

LORD & SMITH
New York, N. Y.
1823

LORD, T.
c. 1825

T·LORD

LORIN, PETER (J)
New York, N. Y.
1751

LORING, ELIJAH
Barnstable, Mass.
1744-1782

 E·Loring E·Loring

LORING, HENRY
Boston, Mass.
1773-1818

 H·L·

LORING, JOSEPH
Boston, Mass.
1743-1815

J.L   J.Loring
J.Loring   JLoring
J.Loring   I.Loring

LOND, ASA
Hartford, Conn.
1765-1823

LOVETT, ROBERT
New York, N. Y.
w. 1824-1838

LOVETT

LOW, FRANCIS
Boston, Mass.
1827

LOW, JOHN J. & CO.
Boston, Mass.
1828

J.J.LOW & CO

LOW, JOHN J.
Salem, Mass.
1821

JJ.LOW

LOWE, JOSHUA (J)
New York, N. Y.
w.c. 1830

I.LOWE   J.LOWE

LOWELL & SENTER
Portland, Me.
c. 1830

LOWELL & SENTER

LOWER, JOSEPH
Philadelphia, Pa.
w. 1803-1831

LOWER

LOWNER, JACOB
Philadelphia, Pa.
1833

LOWNER, WILLIAM
Philadelphia, Pa.
1833

LOWNES, EDWARD
Philadelphia, Pa.
w. 1817-1833

E.LOWNES   E.LOWNES

LOWNES & ERWIN
Philadelphia, Pa.
1816

LOWNES, J. & J. H.
Philadelphia, Pa.
1816

LOWNES, JOSEPH
Philadelphia, Pa.
c. 1754-1820

JL   J.Lownes

LOWNES, JOSIAH H.
Philadelphia, Pa.
d. 1822

IHL   JHL

LOWS, BALL & CO.
Boston, Mass.
1840

LOWS, BALL & COMPANY

PURE
COIN

LOYER, ADRIAN
Savannah, Ga.
1860

LUCET, JAMES
New York, N. Y.
1802

LUKEY, J.
J.LUKEY

LULIS, LAMBERT
New York, N. Y.
1804

LUPP, HENRY
New Brunswick, N. J.
1783
JCLupp

LUPP, LOUIS
New Brunswick, N. J.
Early 19th Century
L Lupp N.Brunswick

LUPP, PETER
New Brunswick, N. J.
w. 1787
P.L

LUPP, S. V.
New Brunswick, N. J.
1815
SV LUPP

LUSCOMB, JOHN G.
Boston, Mass.
1823

LUSSAUR, JOHN
New York, N. Y.
1791

LUZERDER, BENJAMIN
New York, N. Y.
1796

LYELL, DAVID
New York, N. Y.
1699

LYNCH, JOHN
Baltimore, Md.
1761-1848
I·LYNCH ·J·LYNCH·
LYNCH J.LYNCH J D
J LYNCH I·L IL JL

LYNCH & LEONARD
Baltimore, Md.
c. 1840
LYNCH&
LEONARD

LYNDE, THOMAS
Worcester, Mass.
1748-1812
T.LYNDE

LYNG, JOHN
Philadelphia, Pa.
1734
I·L

LYNG, JOHN BURT
New York, N. Y.
w.c. 1761-1780
J·L JBL LYNG N·YORK
LYNG
N.YORK

LYNN, ADAM
Alexandria, Va.
1775-1836

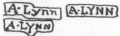

LYTLE, R. A.
Baltimore, Md.
1825

RA LYTLE 10-15

M

MABRID & CO.
New York, N. Y.
1787

MACHON, AUSTIN
Philadelphia, Pa.
1759

MAIN, DAVID
Stonington, Conn.
1752-1843

MAINWARING, THOMAS
New Jersey
1664

MANN, ALEXANDER
Middletown, Conn.
b. 1777, w. 1804

MANNERBACK, WM.
Reading, Pa.
1825

W. MANNERBACK
READING

MANNING, DANIEL
Boston, Mass.
1823

MANNING, JOSEPH
New York, N. Y.
1823

MANNING, SAMUEL
Boston, Mass.
1823

MANSFIELD, ELISHA H.
Norwich, Conn.
b. 1795, w. 1816

MANSFIELD, JOHN
Charlestown, Mass.
1634

MANSFIELD, THOMAS
Philadelphia, Pa.
1804

MARBLE, BENJAMIN
Albany, N. Y.
w.c. 1840-1850

MARBLE, SIMEON
New Haven, Conn.
1777-1856

S.MARBLE

MARCHAND, EVARISTE
New Orleans, La.
1822

MARQUAND & BROS. (J)
New York, N. Y.
w. 1831-1838

Top: salver by John Coney. Center: chafing dish by John Coney. Bottom: salt cup by Charles Le Roux. (*Courtesy of The Metropolitan Museum of Art*)

MARQUAND & CO. (J)
New York, N. Y.
c. 1835

MARQUAND, FREDERICK (J)
New York, N. Y.
w. 1824-1833

F.M. F.MARQUAND

F.M. ☒ ⑪ ©

MARQUAND, ISAAC
New York, N. Y.
w. 1810, *d.* 1815

MARS, S.
c. 1770

S∴Mars

MARSH, THOMAS K.
Paris, Ky.
w. 1830-1850

T.K.MARSH PARISKY

MARSHALL, JOSEPH
Philadelphia, Pa.
1818

MARSHALL & TEMPEST
Philadelphia, Pa.
1813

MARSHALL TEMPEST

MARSHALL, THOMAS H.
Rochester, N. Y.
w. 1832-1852

T. H. MARSHALL

MARSHALL, THOMAS
Troy, N. Y.
1839

MARTIN, ABRAHAM W.
New York, N. Y.
1835

MARTIN, PATRICK (W)
Philadelphia, Pa.
w. 1820-1850

MARTIN, PETER
New York, N. Y.
w. 1756

P.MARTIN PM

MARTIN, PETER II
New York, N. Y.
c. 1825

P.MARTIN

MARTIN, VALENTINE
Boston, Mass.
c. 1845

V.MARTIN BOSTON

MASI, SERAPHIM
Washington, D. C.
1832

MASON, J. D.
Philadelphia, Pa.
1830

J.D.MASON

MATHER & NORTH (W)
New Britain, Conn.
1828

MATHER & NORTH

MATHEY, AUGUSTUS (W)
New York, N. Y.
c. 1825

A.MATHEY

MATLACK, WILLIAM
Philadelphia, Pa.
1828

MATSON, NEWELL
Oswego, N. Y.
1817-1887

 N.MATSON

MAVERICK, D.
New York, N. Y.
1828

DMV

MAVERICK, PETER C.
New York, N. Y.
1755-1811

MAYNARD, R. H.
Buffalo, N. Y.
w. 1826

R·H·MAYNARD

MAYSENHOEDER, C.
Philadelphia, Pa.
1824

McCLYMON, JOHN C.
New York, N. Y.
w.c. 1805-1815

JMcClymon   JMcClymon

McCLYMON, WILLIAM
Schenectady, N. Y.
w. 1800-1815

McClymon

McCOLLIN, T.

T. McCOLLIN

McCONNELL, HUGH
Philadelphia, Pa.
1813

McCONNELL

McCONNELL, THOMAS
Wilmington, Del.
1768-1825

McCORMICK, JOHN
Schenectady, N. Y.
1837

McCREA, ROBERT
Schenectady, N. Y.
1785

McDANIEL, PETER
New York, N. Y.
1743

McDONALD, DANIEL
Philadelphia, Pa.
1828

McDONNOUGH, PATRICK
Philadelphia, Pa.
1811

McDONNOUGH, JOHN
Philadelphia, Pa.
1775

McDOUGALL, WM.
Meredith, N. H.
c. 1825

WM.MCDOUGALL

McDOWELL, WILLIAM H.
Philadelphia, Pa.
1795-1842

Wm.H. McDowell

MCFADDEN, J. B.
Pittsburgh, Pa.
1840

J.B.M FADDEN

MCFARLANE, JOHN
Boston, Mass.
c. 1795

J.M°F   J.M°FARLANE

MCFEE, JOHN
Philadelphia, Pa.
1793

MCFEE, M.
Philadelphia, Pa.
1769

MCFEE & REEDER
Philadelphia, Pa.
c. 1795

M∝R

MCGRAW, DANIEL
Chester, Pa.
1772

MCHARG, ALEXANDER
Albany, N. Y.
1849

MCINTIRE, JAMES
Philadelphia, Pa.
1840

MCINTOSH, JOHN
Ft. Stanwix, Pa.
1761

MCKEEN, HENRY (W)
Philadelphia, Pa.
w. 1823-1850

H.McKEEN

MCKLIMENT, JOHN
New York, N. Y.
1804

MCLAWRENCE, JOHN
New York, N. Y.
1818

MCMAHON, JOHN
Philadelphia, Pa.
1804

MCMASTERS, HUGH A.
Philadelphia, Pa.
w. 1839-1850

H.A.McMASTERS

MCMULLEN, WILLIAM
Philadelphia, Pa.
1791

MCMULLIN & BLACK
Philadelphia, Pa.
1812

McMullin & BLACK

MCMULLIN, JOHN
Philadelphia, Pa.
1765-1843

LM   I McMullin
McMullin   I·MMULLIN

MCNEIL, E.
Troy, N. Y.
c. 1838

E.McNEIL.

Top: Chafing dish by John Burt. Bottom: sauce-boat by Joseph Rich-ardson. (*Courtesy of The Metropolitan Museum of Art*).

McParlin, William
Annapolis, Md.
1780-1850

W.M:P

McPherson, Robert
Philadelphia, Pa.
1831

Mead & Adriance
Ithaca, N. Y., to 1837
St. Louis, Mo., from 1837

MEAD FADRIANCE
ST. LOUIS

Mead, Edmund
St. Louis, Mo.
c. 1850

E.MEAD

Meadows & Co.
Philadelphia, Pa.
1831

MEADOWS&CO PHIA

Mecom, John
New York, N. Y.
1770

Mecum, George
Boston, Mass.
w. 1825-1846

G MECUM

Megear, T. J. (W)
Philadelphia, Pa.
w. 1833-1850

T.J.MEGEAR   STANDARD

Merchant, J.
New York, N. Y.
1795

J.MERCHANT

Meredith, Joseph P. (W)
Baltimore, Md.
w. 1824-1848

J.MEREDITH

Merick, J.
c. 1800

J. MERICK

Merkler, John H.
New York, N. Y.
1780

JHM

Merrick
c. 1820

.MERRICK.

Merrifield, Thomas V. Z.
Albany, N. Y.
1840

Merriman & Bradley
New Haven, Conn.
after 1817

M&B

Merriman, C.
New York, N. Y.
1825

MERRIMAN, MARCUS
New Haven, Conn.
1762-1850

MERRIMAN, MARCUS, & CO.
New Haven, Conn.
1806-1817

MERRIMAN, REUBEN
Litchfield, Conn.
1783-1866

R MERRIMAN

RM

MERRIMAN, SAMUEL
New Haven, Conn.
1769-1805

S.Merriman

MERRIMAN, SILAS
New Haven, Conn.
1734-1805

MERRIMAN & TUTTLE
New Haven, Conn.
From 1802

MERROW, NATHAN
East Hartford, Conn.
1758-1825

MESSINGER, S.
c. 1800

S.MESSINGER

MEYER, JOSEPH
Canton, O.
w. 1840

MICHAELS, JAMES
New York, N. Y.
1820

MIKSCH, JOHN M.
Bethlehem, Pa.
1775

J·M·MIKSCH

MILES, JOHN
Philadelphia, Pa.
1785

MILHE, STEPHEN
Philadelphia, Pa.
1780

MILLAR, JAMES
Boston, Mass.
1832

MILLARD, GEORGE
Philadelphia, Pa.
1816

MILLER, A.

A.MILLER

MILLER, D. B.
Boston, Mass.
1850

DBMILLER

MILLER, I. R.
Philadelphia, Pa.
1810

R MILLER

MILLER, JOHN D.
Charleston, S. Car.
w.c. 1780-1813

MILLER, L. H. & Co.
Baltimore, Md.
c. 1840

MILLER, MATTHEW
Charleston, S. Car.
w.c. 1805-1840

MILLER, PARDON
Providence, R. I.
d. 1800

MILLER, WILLIAM
Philadelphia, Pa.
1814

MILLER, WILLIAM
Charleston, S. Car.
w. 1819

MILLER & SON
Philadelphia, Pa.
1833

MILLNER, THOMAS
Boston, Mass.
1690-1745

MILNE, EDMUND
Philadelphia, Pa.
w. 1761, *d.* 1813

MILNE, F.
New York, N. Y.
1800

MILNE, THOMAS (J)
New York, N. Y.
w. 1796-1815

MILLON, PETER
New York, N. Y.
1820

MILLOUDON, PHILLIPPE
Philadelphia, Pa.
1811

MILLS, EDMUND
Philadelphia, Pa.
1785

MILLS, EDWARD
Philadelphia, Pa.
1794

MILLS, JOHN
Philadelphia, Pa.
1793

MINOTT & AUSTIN
Boston, Mass.
w. 1765-1769

MINOTT, SAMUEL
Boston, Mass.
1732-1803

Top: salt-cellars by Andrew E. Warner. Bottom: salt-cellars by Josiah Austin. (*Courtesy of The Metropolitan Museum of Art*).

MINOTT & SIMPKINS
Boston, Mass.
1769

MINSHALL, WILLIAM
Philadelphia, Pa.
1773

MINTON

MITCHELL, HENRY
Philadelphia, Pa.
1844

MITCHELL, PHINEAS
Boston, Mass.
1812

MITCHELL, WILLIAM
Richmond, Va.
1820

MIX, JAMES
Albany, N. Y.
1817

MIX, VISSCHER
Albany, N. Y.
1849

MOBBS, WILLIAM
Buffalo, N. Y.
1835

MOFFAT, CHARLES H.
New York, N. Y.
1830

MOFFAT, JOHN L.
New York, N. Y.
1815

MOHLER, JACOB
Baltimore, Md.
1744-1773

MONELL & WILLIAMS
New York, N. Y.
c. 1825

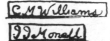

MONK, JAMES
Charleston, S. Car.
w.c. 1797-1809

MONTEITH, J. & R.
Baltimore, Md.
w. 1814-1849

MONTEITH, JOHN
Baltimore, Md.
w. 1814-1849

MONTEITH, ROBERT
Baltimore, Md.
w. 1814-1849

MOOD & EWAN
> Charleston, S. Car.
> *c.* 1824

MOOD, J. & P.
> Charleston, S. Car.
> *w.c.* 1834-1841
> ┌─────────────┐
> │ J.&P.MOOD │
> └─────────────┘

MOOD, JOHN
> Charleston, S. Car.
> *w.* 1816-1864
> ┌─────────┐
> │ JMOOD │
> └─────────┘

MOOD, JOSEPH
> Charleston, S. Car.
> 1806
> ┌───┐ ┌────────┐ ┌────────┐
> │ I │ │ MOOD │ │ IMOOD │
> └───┘ └────────┘ └────────┘

MOOD, PETER, SR.
> Charleston, S. Car.
> *w.* 1785-1821
> ┌──────────┐ ┌────┐ ┌────────┐
> │ P.MOOD │ │ PM │ │ MOOD │
> └──────────┘ └────┘ └────────┘

MOOD, PETER, JR.
> Charleston, S. Car.
> *w.c.* 1819, *c.* 1842
> ┌──────────────┐
> │ P.MOOD.JR │
> └──────────────┘

MOORE & BREWER
> New York, N.Y.
> *w.* 1824
> ┌──────────────────────┐
> │ MOORE & BREWER │
> └──────────────────────┘

MOORE & BROWN
> New York, N.Y.
> 1833

MOORE, CHARLES
> Philadelphia, Pa.
> *w.* 1803-1809
> ┌─────────────┐
> │ C.MOORE │
> └─────────────┘

MOORE & FERGUSON
> Philadelphia, Pa.
> 1804
> ┌────────────────────────┐
> │ MOORE & FERGUSON │
> └────────────────────────┘

MOORE, H.
> Philadelphia, Pa.
> ┌─────────────┐
> │ H.MOORE │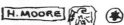
> └─────────────┘

MOORE & HIBBARD
> ┌────────┐
> │ M&H │
> └────────┘

MOORE, JARED L. (W)
> New York, N.Y.
> *w.* 1825-1840
> ┌───────────────┐ ┌──────────┐
> │ JL.MOORE │ │ MOORE │
> └───────────────┘ └──────────┘

MOORE, JOHN C.
> New York, N.Y.
> 1844
> ┌─────────┐
> │ J.C.M. │
> └─────────┘

MOORE, ROBERT
> Maryland
> 1778

MOORE, THOMAS
> Philadelphia, Pa.
> 1805

MORGAN
> *c.* 1860
> MORGAN

MORGAN, ELIJAH
Poughkeepsie, N. Y.
w. 1807-1824

[E MORGAN][POUGHKEEPSIE]

MORGAN, JOHN
Philadelphia, Pa.
1813

MORMAGEA, MICHAEL
Philadelphia, Pa.
1816

MORRELL, WILLIAM M. (J)
New York, N. Y.
w. 1828-1834

[W. MORRELL]

MORRIS, JOHN
New York, N. Y.
1796

MORRIS, SILVESTER
New York, N. Y.
1709-1783

[SM]

MORRIS, WILLIAM H.
1759

MORRISON, ISRAEL
Philadelphia, Pa.
1823

MORSE, DAVID
Boston, Mass.
1798

MORSE, HAZEN
Boston, Mass.
1815

MORSE, J. H.
Boston, Mass.
1795

[J.H.MORSE]

MORSE, MOSES
Boston, Mass.
w. 1815-1830

[M.MORSE] [MORSE]

MORSE, NATHANIEL
Boston, Mass.
c. 1685-1748

MORSE, OBADIAH
Boston, Mass.
w. 1733

MORSE, STEPHEN
Boston, Mass.
1764

[MORSE]

MOSELY, DAVID
Boston, Mass.
1753-1812

[DM] [DMoseley]
[D.Moseley]

MOSELY, JOSEPH
New York, N. Y.
1830

MOSES, JACOB
Birmingham, Ala.
1768

[MOSES]

Porringer by
Benjamin Burt

Porringer by
John Burr

Porringer by Benjamin Burt

(*All photos Courtesy of The
Metropolitan Museum of Art*).

MOSES, M.
Boston, Mass.
1830

MOSES, ISAAC N.
Derby, Conn.
1781

MOTT, J. S.
New York, N. Y.
w. 1790-1830

J.MOTT   JMOTT

J.S.MOTT

MOTT, J. & W. (W)
New York, N. Y.
1789

MOTT'S

MOTT, JORDAN (W)
New York, N. Y.
w. 1815-1835

MOULINAR, JOHN
New York, N. Y.
From 1744

IM   IM

MOULTON, ABEL
Newburyport, Mass.
1815

A·MOULTON

MOULTON & BRADBURY
Newburyport, Mass.
1796

MOULTON   B

MOULTON & DAVIS
Newburyport, Mass.
1824-1830

M & D

MOULTON, EBENEZER S.
Boston, Mass.
w. 1796-1817

MOULTON

E.S.MOULTON

E.S.Moulton

MOULTON, ENOCH
Portland, Me.
1801

MOULTON, EDWARD S.
Rochester, N. H.
1778-1855

MOULTON, JOSEPH
Newburyport, Mass.
1680

MOULTON, JOSEPH M.
Newburyport, Mass.
1744-1816

MOULTON

J·M   J·M   IM   J·M

I·MOULTON

MOULTON, JOSEPH M., JR.
Newburyport, Mass.
1814-1903

J.MOULTON.

J.MOULTON

MOULTON, WILLIAM
Newburyport, Mass.
1720-1793

W.MOULTON

MOULTON, WILLIAM II
Newburyport, Mass.
1772-1860

W·M

MULFORD, JOHN H.
Albany, N. Y.
1835

MULFORD & WENDELL
Albany, N. Y.
1842-1850

MULFORD WENDELL

MULLIGAN, H.
Philadelphia, Pa.
1840

H MULLIGAN
4th 21st ST PHILA

MUMFORD, HENRY B.
Providence, R. I.
1813

MUMFORD

MUNGER, ASA
Herkimer, N. Y.
w. 1810-1818

A.MUNGER

MUNGER, A., & SON
Auburn, N. Y.
c. 1825

A.MUNGER & SON   AUBURN

MUNROE, JAMES
Barnstable, Mass.
1784-1879

I·MUNROE   I·MUNROE

James Munroe   PureCoin

MUNROE, NATHANIEL
Baltimore, Md.
1777-1861

N.MUNROE   N.MUNROE

MUNSELL, G. C.

G.C.MUNSELL PURE COIN

MUNSON, AMOS
New Haven, Conn.
1753-1785

MUNSON, CORNELIUS
Wallingford, Conn.
b. 1742

MURDOCK & ANDREWS
Utica, N. Y.
1822-1849

MURDOCK, JAMES, & CO.
Utica, N. Y.
1826-1838

JAMES MURDOCK & CO

MURDOCK, JOHN
Philadelphia, Pa.
c. 1780

I.M.   J Murdock

MURPHY, JAMES
Boston, Mass., 1816
Philadelphia, Pa.
w. 1828-1846

J.MURPHY

MUSGRAVE, JAMES
Philadelphia, Pa.
1795

Musgrave

MYER, H. B.
Newburgh, N. Y.
Buffalo, N. Y.
w. 1826-1848

HBMyer

MYERS, ALBERT
Philadelphia, Pa.
1837

MYERS & JACOB
Philadelphia, Pa.
1839

MYERS, JOHN
Philadelphia, Pa.
w. 1773-1804

 I·MYERS JMyers

MYERS, MYER
New York, N. Y.
1723-1795

 MM M·M Myers
Myers

MYGATT, COMFORT S.
Danbury, Conn.
1763-1823, *w.* to 1807

MYGATT, DAVID
Danbury, Conn.
1777-1822

DM DMYGATT
D·MYGATT

MYGATT, ELY
Danbury, Conn.
1742-1807

MYSENDHENDER,
Philadelphia, Pa.
1813

N

NAGLES, JOHN
Philadelphia, Pa.
1748

NEALL, DANIEL
Milford, Del.
1784-1846

D. NEALL

NEEDLES (NEEDELS) WILLIAM
Easton, Md.
w. 1798-1818

W.NEEDELS

NELSON, JOHN
Portsmouth, N. H.
1780

IN

NEUSS, JAN
Philadelphia, Pa.
1698

NEVILL, RICHARD
Boston, Mass.
1674

NEVILL, RICHARD
Boston, Mass.
1764

NEWBERRY, EDWIN C.
Brooklyn, N. Y.
from *c.* 1828

NEWCOMB, H. K.
Watertown, N. Y.
w. 1821-1850

[H.K.NEWCOMB]

NEWHALL, DUDLEY
Salem, Mass.
1730

NEWKIRKE (NIEWKIRKE), J.
New York, N. Y.
1716

[I·N] [I·N] [I·K]

NEWMAN, TIMOTHY H.
Groton, Mass.
1778-1812

[T.H.Newman]

[Newman] [Newman]

NEWTON & REED (R)

[NEWTON & REED]

NICHOLAS, WILLIAM S.
Newport, R. I.
1785-1871

NICHOLS & SALISBURY
Charleston, S. Car.
c. 1845

NICHOLS, BASSET
Providence, R. I.
1815

[NICHOLS] ⊙ ⊕ ⊙

NICHOLS, H.
19th Century

[H.M.NICHOLS]

[H.NICHOLS]

NICHOLS, WILLIAM S.
Newport, R. I.
1785-1871

[W.S·N] [NICHOLS] [WSN]

[NICHOLS] [W.S.N]

NIXON, RICHARD
Philadelphia, Pa.
w. 1820-1835

[R.NIXON]

NOBLE, JOSEPH
Portland, Me.
1823

NORCROSS, NEHEMIAH
Boston, Mass.
w.c. 1796

[NN]

NORRIS, GEORGE
Philadelphia, Pa.
1779

NORTH, W. B. & CO.
New York, N. Y.
1823

[W.B.NORTH&CO.]

NORTH, WILLIAM B. (J) (W)
New York, N. Y.
1787-1838

[WBNORTH&CO] [W.B.N]

NORTHEE, DAVID I.
Salem, Mass.
w. 1770, *d.* 1778

NORTHEY, ABIJAH
Salem, Mass.
1775

NORTON, ANDREW
Goshen, Conn.
1765-1838

NORTON, BENJAMIN
Boston, Mass.
1810

NORTON, BENJ. R.
Syracuse, N. Y.
c. 1842

NORTON, C. C.
Hartford, Conn.
1820

NORTON, SAMUEL
Hingham, Mass.
1795

NORTON, THOMAS
Farmington, Conn.
1773-1834

NORTON & PITKIN
Hartford, Conn.
c. 1825

NORTON & SEYMOUR
Syracuse, N. Y.
c. 1850

NORWOOD, RICHARD
New York, N. Y.
1774

NOXON, MARTIN
Edenton, N. C.
1780-1814

NOYES, JOHN
Boston, Mass.
1674-1749

NOYES, SAMUEL
Norwich, Conn.
1747-1781

NUSZ, FREDERICK
Frederick, Md.
1819

NUTTALL, JOSEPH
Maryland
1778

NYS, JOHANNIS
Philadelphia, Pa.
w.c. 1695-1723

Silver bowl of characteristic New York design, made by Cornelius
Kierstede. (*Courtesy of The Metropolitan Museum of Art*).

Left: porringer by John de Nise. Right: porringer by Samuel Vernon.
(*Courtesy of The Metropolitan Museum of Art*).

O

OAKES, FREDERICK
Hartford, Conn.
w. 1810, *d.* 1825

OAKES OAKES

OAKES, H.

H. Oakes.

OAKES & SPENCER
Hartford, Conn.
1814

O&S

ODELL, LAWRENCE
New York, N. Y.
1830

OERTELT, CHARLES E.
Philadelphia, Pa.
1831

OGIER, JOHN
New York, N. Y.
1791

OGILVIE, JOHN
New York, N. Y.
w.c. 1760

I*OGILVIE

OLIVER, ANDREW
Boston, Mass.
b.c. 1722

A·OLIVER AO

OLIVER, DANIEL
Philadelphia, Pa.
1805

D.OLIVER

OLIVER, PETER
Boston, Mass.
1682-1712

PO PO

OLIVIER, PETER
Philadelphia, Pa.
d. 1798

P.O P.O

OLMSTED, NATHANIEL
Farmington, Conn.
1785-1860
New Haven, Conn., *w.* 1826

N.OLMSTED P

OLMSTED, N. & SON
Farmington, Conn.
1847

N.OLMSTED & SON P

ONCLEBAGH, GARRET
New York, N. Y.
1670-1732

B GO

OSBORN, WILLIAM
Providence, R. I.
mid 19th Century

William Osborn

OSGOOD, JOHN
Boston, Mass.
w. 1795-1817

J:OSGOOD

OSTOFF, ANDREW
Baltimore, Md.
c. 1810
[A.OSTHOFF]

OTIS, JOHN
Barnstable, Mass.
1706

OTIS, JONATHAN
Newport, R. I., 1723-1791
Middleton, Conn., from 1775
(J.O) (J.Otis) (Otis)
(J.Otis) (OTIS) (J.OTIS)

OTT, DANIEL
New York, N. Y.
1792

OTT, GEORGE
Norfolk, Va.
1806
(J.Ott) (Ott.)

OVERIN, RICHARD
New York, N. Y.
1701

OWEN, JESSE
Philadelphia, Pa.
w.c. 1794-1848
[OWEN] [J⁰⁰OWEN]

OWEN, JOHN
Philadelphia, Pa.
w. 1804-1831
[I·OWEN]

P

PADDY, SAMUEL
Boston, Mass.
1667

PAINTER, JOHN
Philadelphia, Pa.
1735

PALMER & BACHELDER
Boston, Mass.
1850
[PALMER & BATCHELDER]

PALMER & CLAPP
New York, N. Y.
1823

PALMER & HINSDALE
New York, N. Y.
1815

PALMER, JAMES
New York, N. Y.
1815

PALMER & NEWCOMB

PANCOAST, SAMUEL
Philadelphia, Pa.
w. 1785-1795
[PANCOAST]

PANGBORN & BRINSMAID
Burlington, Vt.
1833
[P.&B.]

PARADICE, WILLIAM A.
Philadelphia, Pa.
1799

PARASET, WILLIAM
Philadelphia, Pa.
1811

PARHAM, WILLIAM
Philadelphia, Pa.
w. 1785-*c.* 1795

PARIE, JOSEPH
Philadelphia, Pa.
1811

PARISIEN, OTTO P.
New York, N. Y.
c. 1790

PARKER, ALLEN (J)
New York, N. Y.
c. 1818

PARKER, DANIEL
Boston, Mass.
1726-1785

PARKER, GEORGE
Baltimore, Md.
1804

PARKER, ISAAC
Deerfield, Mass.
1780

PARKER, JOSEPH
Princeton, N. J.
1785

PARKER, RICHARD
Philadelphia, Pa.
1785

PARKER, WILLIAM H.
New York, N. Y.
1835

PARKMAN, CHARLES
Boston, Mass.
1790

PARKMAN, JOHN
Boston, Mass.
1738

PARKMAN, THOMAS
Boston, Mass.
1793

PARKS, JOHN
New York, N. Y.
1791

PARMELE, JAMES
Durham, Conn.
1763-1828

PARMELE, SAMUEL
Guilford, Conn.
1737-1803

PARROTT, T.
Boston, Mass.
c. 1760

PARRY, MARTIN
Kittery, Me.
1756-1802

[PARRY]

PARRY & MUSGRAVE
Philadelphia, Pa.
w. 1793

[P&M]

PARRY, ROWLAND
Philadelphia, Pa.
w.c. 1790-1796

[RPARRY]

PARSONS, JOHN
Boston, Mass.
1780

[JPARSONS] [PARSONS]

PASCAL, WILLIAM
Philadelphia, Pa.
1765

PATON, A.
Boston, Mass.
1850

PATTERSON, GEORGE
New York, N. Y.
1835

PATTERSON, JOHN
Annapolis, Md.
1751

[I·P]

PATTIT, THOMAS
New York, N. Y.
1796

PATTON, THOMAS
Philadelphia, Pa.
1824

PAXSON, JOHN A.
Philadelphia, Pa.
1810

PEABODY, JOHN
Enfield, Conn.
1799

[J.PEABODY]

PEALE, CHARLES W.
Philadelphia, Pa.
1765

PEAR, EDWARD
Boston, Mass.
w. 1836-1850

[E P] [E.P.]

PEAR & BACALL
Boston, Mass.
1850

PEARCE, WILLIAM
Norfolk, Va.
1820

PEARSE, SAMUEL
New York, N. Y.
1783

PEARSON, JOHN
New York, N. Y.
1791

PEARSON, M. & T.

M&T.PEARSON

PECK, A. G.

A.G PECK

PECK, B.
Connecticut
c. 1820

BPECK

PECK, LAWRENCE M.
Philadelphia, Pa.
1837

PECK, TIMOTHY
Middletown, Conn.
Litchfield, Conn., w. 1791
1765-1818

PEDASY, S.
Philadelphia, Pa.
1810

PEIRI, JOSEPH
Philadelphia, Pa.
1811

PELL, EMMET T. (J)
New York, N. Y.
w. 1824-1841

E.T.PELL

PELLETREAU, BENNETT & COOKE
New York, N. Y.
1815

PELLETREAU, ELIAS
Southampton, N. Y.
New York, N. Y., from 1748
1726-1810

EP   E·P

PELLETREAU, JOHN
Southampton, N. Y.
1785

PELLETREAU, MALTBY
New York, N. Y.
w. 1815-1835

M·P

PELLETREAU & RICHARDS
New York, N. Y.
1825

WSP   IR

PELLETREAU & UPSON
New York, N. Y.
1818

P&U

Two-handled bowls of late 17th Century, New York design, makers unknown.

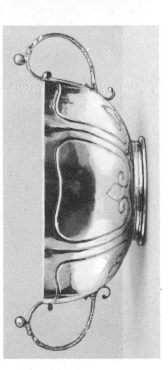

Left: two-handled bowl by Jacob Boelen. Right: dram cup by Jacob Boelen. (*All photos Courtesy of The Metropolitan Museum of Art*).

PELLETREAU & VAN WYCK
New York, N. Y.
1815

W.S.PELLETREAU S.VAN.WYCK

PELLETREAU, WM. S.
Southampton, N. Y.
1786-1842

W.S.PELLETREAU

PEPPER, HENRY I.
Philadelphia, Pa.
1766

H.I.PEPPER H.I.PEPPER

PEPPER, HENRY J.
Philadelphia, Pa.
w.c. 1828-1850

H.J.PEPPER

PEPPER, HENRY J., & SON
(W)
Philadelphia, Pa.
w. 1846-1850

 H.I. PEPPER & SON

PERKINS, HOUGHTON
Boston, Mass.
1762

H·P

PERKINS, ISAAC
Charlestown, Mass.
1707

PERKINS, JACOB
Newburyport, Mass.
1766-1849

 J.PERKINS

PERKINS, JOSEPH
Little Rest, R. I.
1749-1789

J.PERKINS

PERKINS, T.
Boston, Mass.
1810

T.PERKINS

PERPIGNAN, PETER
Philadelphia, Pa.
1809

PERPIGNAN & VARNIER
Philadelphia, Pa.
1800

PERREAUX, PETER
Philadelphia, Pa.
1797

P.P P.P

PERRET & SANDER
New York, N. Y.
1810

PERRET, AUGUSTA
New York, N. Y.
1801

PERRY, THOMAS
Westerly, R. I.

T.PERRY

PETERS, JAMES
Philadelphia, Pa.
w. 1821-1850

J.PETERS

PETERS, J., & CO.
Philadelphia, Pa.
c. 1830
J PETERS & Co.

PETERS, R.
Philadelphia, Pa.
1802

PETERSON, HENRY
Philadelphia, Pa.
1783
H.P.

PETIT, MATTHEW
New York, N. Y.
1811
MP

PETRIE, ALEXANDER
Charleston, S. Car.
w. 1745-1765
A.P.

PETTIT, THOMAS
New York, N. Y.
1791

PHELPS, CHARLES H.
Bainbridge, N. Y.
1825
CH PHELPS

PHELPS, JEDEDIAH
Gt. Barrington, Vt.
1781

PHILIP & YVER
Philadelphia, Pa.
1796

PHILIPS, JAMES D.
Cleveland, Ohio
1829
JAⁱD.PHILIPS

PHILLIPE, JOSEPH
Baltimore, Md.
1796

PHILLIPS, SAMUEL
Salem, Mass.
1658-1721
SP

PHINNEY & MEAD
1825
P&M

PHYFE, WILLIAM
Boston, Mass.
1830

PICKERING, CHARLES
Philadelphia, Pa.
1683

PIERCE, HART
New York, N. Y.
1835

PIERCE, JOHN
Boston, Mass.
1810
PIERCE

PIERCE, O.
Boston, Mass.
1824
O.PIERCE   O.PIERCE

PIERPONT, BENJAMIN
Boston, Mass.
1730-1797

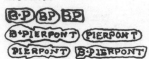

PIERSON, PHILLIP
New York, N. Y.
1798

PIKE, H.
19th Century

PINCHIN, WILLIAM
Philadelphia, Pa.
1779

PINTO, JOSEPH
New York, N. Y.
1758

PITKIN, HENRY
E. Hartford, Conn.
1834

PITKIN, HORACE E.
Hartford, Conn.
1832

PITKIN, JAMES F.
E. Hartford, Conn.
1834

PITKIN, JOHN O.
E. Hartford, Conn.
Vicksburg, Tenn., w. 1834-1837
1803-1891

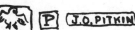

PITKIN, J. O. & W.
E. Hartford, Conn.
1826-1840

PITKIN & NORTON
Hartford, Conn.
1825

PITKIN, WALTER M.
E. Hartford, Conn.
1808-1885

PITKIN, WILLIAM J.
E. Hartford, Conn.
1820

PITKIN, WILLIAM L.
E. Hartford, Conn.
1825

PITKINS, JAMES
Hartford, Conn.
1812

PITMAN, BENJAMIN
Providence, R. I.
1825

PITMAN & DODGE
Providence, R. I.
1795

PITMAN & DORRANCE
Providence, R. I.
c. 1795

PITMAN, I.

Baltimore, Md.
1785

PITMAN, JOHN K.

Providence, R. I.
1805

PITMAN, SAUNDERS

Providence, R. I.
1732-1804

PITMAN, WILLIAM R.

New Bedford, Mass.
1835

[WRP]

PITTS, A.

PITTS, RICHARD

Philadelphia, Pa.
w. 1741-1745
Charleston, S. Car.
1746

[Pitts]

PLACE, DANIEL

Rochester, N. Y., 1827
Ithaca, N. Y., c. 1840

[PLACE]

PLAIN, EDWARD

New York, N. Y.
1835

PLANQUET, GREGORY

New York, N. Y.
1797

PLATT & BROTHER

New York, N. Y.
1820

[PLATT & BROTHER]

[PLATT & BRO]

PLATT & BROTHERS

New York, N. Y.
w. 1836-1846

[PLATT & BROTHERS]

PLATT, GEORGE W.

New York, N. Y.
1820

PLATT, G. W. & N. C.

New York, N. Y.
1820

[GW.&N.C.PLATT]

[PLATT & BROTHER]

PLATT, JAMES

New York, N. Y.
1835

PLATT, M. C.

New York, N. Y.
1820

PLUMMER, J. F.

[J.F.PLUMMER]

POINCIGNON, FRANCIS

Philadelphia, Pa.
1798

POINCY, PETER

Philadelphia, Pa.
1813

POINTE, JAMES
Philadelphia, Pa.
1813

POINTE & TANGUY
Philadelphia, Pa.
1818

POISSENOT, N. J.
Philadelphia, Pa.
1806

POISSONIER, FRANCIS
Philadelphia, Pa.
1795

POLAND, P.
Philadelphia, Pa.
1837

POLHAMUS, J.
New York, N. Y.
1802

POLLARD, H. N.

H.N.POLLARD & Co.

H.N.POLLARD

POLLARD, WILLIAM
Boston, Mass.
1687-1746

W·P W·P

PONCET, LEWIS
Baltimore, Md.
w. 1800-1822

L PONCET

PONS, THOMAS
Boston, Mass.
w. 1789-1805

PONS. PONS PONS

POOLE, WILLIAM
Wilmington, Del.
1764-1846

W.P

POOR, NATHANIEL
Boston, Mass.
1829

PORTER, F. W.
New York, N. Y.
1820

F.W.PORTER

PORTER, HENRY C.
New York, N. Y.
1820

PORTER, HENRY, & CO.
Boston, Mass.
c. 1830

H.PORTER & CO

PORTER, JOSEPH S.
Utica, New York
1783-1862

S Porter

POSEY, FREDERICK J.
Hagerstown, Md.
w. 1820-1850

F.J.POSEY

POST, SAMUEL
New London, Conn.
b. 1736, c. 1783

POTTER, NILES
Westerly, R. I.

1770   1720   1790   1800

1790   1780   1730

1800   1730   1725

1700   1810   1700

POTTER, J. O. & J. R.
Providence, R. I.
w. 1810-1824

POTWINE, JOHN
Boston, Mass.
Hartford, Conn., after 1737
1698-1792

POTWINE & WHITING
Hartford, Conn.
1761

POUPARD, JAMES
Boston, Mass.
1751

POUTREAU, ABRAHAM
New York, N. Y.
b.c. 1700, *w.* 1726

POWELL, C. F.
Boston, Mass.
1746

POWELSON, CHARLES
Albany, N. Y.
1840

PRATT, HENRY
Philadelphia, Pa.
1708-1749

PRATT, NATHAN
Essex, Conn.
1772-1842

PRATT, PHINEAS
Lyme, Conn.
1747-1813

PRATT, SETH
Lyme, Conn.
1741-1802

PRESCOT, HENRY
Keeseville, N. Y.
c. 1830

PRESTON, S. L.
Philadelphia, Pa.
1850

PRICE, BENJAMIN
Boston, Mass.
1767

PRICE, HENRY P.
Philadelphia, Pa.
1810

PRICE, JOHN
Lancaster, Pa.
1764

PRIE, P.
  c. 1780

PRINCE, JOB
  Milford, Conn.
  c. 1680-1703

PURSE, WILLIAM
  Charleston, S. Car.
  w.c. 1785-1825

PURSELL, HENRY
  New York, N. Y.
  1775

PUTNAM, EDWARD
  Boston, Mass.
  c. 1825

PUTNAM & LOW
  Boston, Mass.
  1822

PUTNAM, RUFUS
  Albany, N. Y.
  1814

PUTNEY, REUBEN H.
  Watertown, N. Y.
  c. 1825

Q

QUIMBY, M.
  19th Century

QUINCY, DANIEL
  Braintree, Mass.
  1651

QUINTARD, PETER
  New York, N. Y.
  So. Norwalk, Conn., 1737
  1699-1762

R

RABETH, JAMES
  New York, N. Y.
  1835

RAIT, DAVID
  New York, N. Y.
  1835

RAIT, ROBERT (J)
  w. 1836-1855

RALSTON, WILLIAM
  Ashland, O.
  w. 1840-1850

RAPP, W. D.
Philadelphia, Pa.
w. 1828-1850

RASCH, ANTHONY
Philadelphia, Pa.
1807

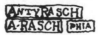

RASCH, ANTHONY & CO.
Philadelphia, Pa.
1820

A RASCH&CO

RASCH, W. A.
New Orleans, La.
1830

W.A.RASCH NEW ORLEANS

RASCH & WILLIG
Philadelphia, Pa.
1819

RATH, FREDERICK (W)
New York, N. Y.
w. 1840

F. RATH

RAVEE, XAVIER
Philadelphia, Pa.
1796

RAYMOND, JOHN
Boston, Mass.
1775

RAYNES, JOSEPH
Lowell, Mass.
1835

JOSEPH RAYNES

REDON, CLAUDIUS (J)
New York, N. Y.
w. 1828

 C. REDON

REED, A. G., & CO.
Nassau, N. H.
1835

REED, I., & SON (W)
Philadelphia, Pa.
w. 1830-1850

IR&S I.REED&SON

REED, ISAAC
Stamford, Conn.
b. 1746, *w.* 1776

REED, JONATHAN
Boston, Mass.
w. 1725-1740

IR

REED, LEWIS
New York, N. Y.
1810

REED, O., & CO. (W)
Philadelphia, Pa.
c. 1841

O.REED&CO

REED, OSMAN
Philadelphia, Pa.
w. 1831-1841

O.REED PHILA

REED, STEPHEN (J)
Philadelphia, Pa.
w. 1846

[SREED] [SREED]

REEDER, ABNER
Philadelphia, Pa.
w. 1793-1800

[A·REEDER]

REEDER, JOHN
Philadelphia, Pa.
1835

REEVE, G.
c. 1825

[G·REEVE]

REEVE, JOSEPH
Newburgh, N. Y.
w. 1803-1828

[J.Reeve]

REEVES, ENOS
Charleston, S. C.
1753-1807

[REEVES]

REEVES, J. F.
Baltimore, Md.
c. 1835

[J.F.REEVES] [S] [D]

REEVES, STEPHEN
Burlington, N. J.
w. 1766-1776

[SReeves]

REVERE, EDWARD
Boston, Mass.
w. 1796, d. 1803

REVERE, JOSEPH W.
Boston, Mass., 1798
Canton, Ohio, 1801

REVERE, PAUL, SR.
Boston, Mass.
1702-1754

[PR] [P.Revere]
[P.REVERE]

REVERE, PAUL
Boston, Mass.
1735-1818

[PR] [PR]
[REVERE] [·REVERE]

REVERE, PAUL, III
Boston, Mass.
1760-1813

REVERE & SON
Boston, Mass.
1796

REVERE, THOMAS
Boston, Mass.
1739-1817

[TR]

REYNOLDS, JOHN
Hagerstown, Md.
1770-1832

[IR] [IR] [Jr Reynolds]

REYNOLDS, THEODORE J.
Philadelphia, Pa.
1835

RICE, HENRY P.
Albany, N. Y.
w. 1815-1830

[H.P.RICE] [†] [⊛] [R]

RICE, JOSEPH

Baltimore, Md.
1784

RICE, JOSEPH T.

Albany, N. Y.
w.c. 1820-1850

RICH, OBADIAH

Boston, Mass.
w.c. 1830-1850

RICHARDS, SAMUEL

Philadelphia, Pa.
1770

RICHARDS, SAMUEL R.

Philadelphia, Pa.
w. 1793-1818

RICHARDS, STEPHEN

New York, N. Y.
w. 1815-1822

RICHARDS, THOMAS (W)

New York, N. Y.
w. 1815-1829

RICHARDS & WILLIAMSON

Philadelphia, Pa.
w. 1793-1800

RICHARDSON, FRANCIS

Philadelphia, Pa.
1681-1729

RICHARDSON, FRANCIS JR.

Philadelphia, Pa.
b. 1708

RICHARDSON, JOSEPH

Philadelphia, Pa.
1711-1784

RICHARDSON, JOSEPH, JR.

Philadelphia, Pa.
1752-1831

RICHARDSON, JOS. & NATHANIEL

Philadelphia, Pa.
w.c. 1771-1791

RICHARDSON, NATHANIEL

Philadelphia, Pa.
1754-1827

RICHARDSON, RICHARD

Philadelphia, Pa.
1793

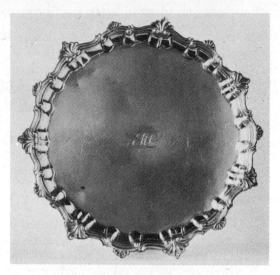

Salver by Thomas Hammersley.

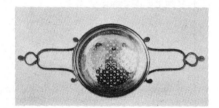 

Left: lemon strainer by John Coburn. Right: porringer by
Benjamin Burt.

Left: candlestick by Jacob Hurd. Right: basket, late 18th century. (*All
photos Courtesy of the Metropolitan Museum of Art*).

RICHMOND, FRANKLIN
Providence, R. I.
1815

[F.RICHMOND]

RICHMOND, G. & A.
Providence, R. I.
1815

RICHMOND, THOMAS
Waterford, N. Y.
w. 1807

[RICHMOND]

RIDGEWAY, JOHN
Boston, Mass.
1780-1851

[J:RIDGWAY]

RIDOUT, GEORGE
New York, N. Y.
from 1743

[GR]

RIED, JOHAN
Philadelphia, Pa.
1810

RIELLY, BERNARD
New York, N. Y.
1835

RIGGS, B. M.
Paris, Ky.
c. 1825-1840

[B.M.RIGGS]

RIGGS, GEORGE W.
Baltimore, Md.
1777-1864

[GR] [Riggs] [RIGGS]
[RIGGS]

RIGGS & GRIFFITH
Baltimore, Md.
1816

[R&G]

RIGGS, RICHARD
Philadelphia, Pa.
d. 1819

[RR] [Riggs]

RIKER, PETER
New York, N. Y.
w. 1802-1814

[P.RIKER]

RIKER & ALEXANDER
New York, N. Y.
1800

RITTER, MICHAEL
New York, N. Y.
1786

RITTER, RICHARD
New York, N. Y.
c. 1790

ROATH, ROSWELL W.
Norwich, Conn.
b. 1805, w. 1826

ROBBINS, ELISHA
Philadelphia, Pa.
1831

ROBERT, CHRISTOPHER
New York, N. Y.
1708-1783

ROBERTS, FREDERICK
Boston, Mass.
1770

ROBERTS & LEE
Boston, Mass.
1775

ROBERTS, MICHAEL
New York, N. Y.
1786

ROBERTSON, ALEXANDER
Philadelphia, Pa.
1740

ROBERTSON, ROBERT
Philadelphia, Pa.
1777

ROBINSON, ANTHONY W.
Philadelphia, Pa.
1798

ROBINSON, BENJAMIN
Philadelphia, Pa.
1818

ROBINSON, E.
c. 1780

ROBINSON, HANNAH
Wilmington, Del.
1845

ROBINSON, ISRAEL
Philadelphia, Pa.
1840

ROBINSON & HARWOOD
Philadelphia, Pa.
1814

ROBINSON, JOHN
Wilmington, Del.
1812-1867

ROBINSON, O.
New Haven, Conn.
c. 1800

ROCKWELL, EDWARD
New York, N. Y.
w. 1807-1825

ROCKWELL, SAMUEL (W)
New York, N. Y.
w. 1834-1841

ROCKWELL, THOMAS (W)
Norwalk, Conn.
w. 1775-1795

RODIER, PETER G.
New York, N. Y.
1825

ROE, JAMES
Kingston, N. Y.
1770

ROE, WILLIAM
Kingston, N. Y.
c. 1805

ROE & STOLLENWERCK
New York, N. Y.
1800

ROFF,
New York, N. Y.
1813

ROGERS, AUGUSTUS
Boston, Mass.
1818

ROGERS, DANIEL
Newport, R. I.
1753-1792

ROGERS, DANIEL
New York, N. Y.
1835

ROGERS, JOSEPH
Newport, R. I.
Hartford, Conn., from 1803
d. 1825

ROGERS & WENDT
Boston, Mass.
1850

ROGERS, WILLIAM
Hartford, Conn.
1801-1873

ROGERS, WILLIAM & SON
Hartford, Conn.
1850

ROHR, JOHN A.
Philadelphia, Pa.
1807

ROLLINGSON, WILLIAM
New York, N. Y.
1783

ROMNEY, JOHN
New York, N. Y.
1770

ROOSEVELT, NICHOLAS
New York, N. Y.
1715-1771

ROOT, CHAS. B.
Raleigh, N. Car.
1818-1903

ROOT, L. M. & A. C. (R)

Pittsfield, Mass.
c. 1830

L.M. & A.C. ROOT

ROOT, W. N. & BRO.

New Haven, Conn.
1850

W.N.ROOT & BROTHER

ROSE, ANTHONY

New York, N. Y.
1755

ROSHORE, JOHN

New York, N. Y.
1792

ROSHORE & PRIME

New York, N. Y.
1825

ROSS, JOHN

Baltimore, Md.
1756-1798

I·R   I·R

ROSS, ROBERT

Frederika, Del.
1789

R.R

ROSWELL, BARTHOLOMEW

Hartford, Conn.
1805

ROTH, NELSON

Utica, N. Y.
w. 1837-1857

N.ROTH-UTICA

ROUND, JOHN

Portsmouth, N. H.
1634

ROUSE, ANTHONY

Philadelphia, Pa.
1807

ROUSE, SIDNEY

Rochester, N. Y.
c. 1850

ROUSE, WILLIAM

Boston, Mass.
1639-1705

WR   WR   W.R   WR

ROUSE, WILLIAM M.

Charleston, S. C.
w. 1831-c. 1875

W.M.ROUSE

ROYALSTON, JOHN

Boston, Mass.
1770

I R

RUDD, J. & Co. (J)

New York, N. Y.
w. 1834-1841

 J.RUDD & Co

RULE,

Massachusetts
1780·

Rule

RUMRILL, A. & Co. (J)

New York, N. Y.
c. 1835

A. RUMRILL & Co.

RUMSEY, C.

C. RUMSEY

RUSSELL, DANIEL
Newport, R. I.
1735

DR DR

RUSSELL, DANIEL
Newport, R. I.
1792

RUSSELL, GEORGE
Philadelphia, Pa.
1831

RUSSELL, JOHN H.
New York, N. Y.
c. 1795

J·H·R

RUSSELL, JONATHAN
Ashford, Conn.
b. 1770, w. 1804

·RUSSEL

RUSSELL, JOSEPH
Barnstable, Mass.
c. 1725

RUSSELL, MOODY
Barnstable, Mass.
1694-1761

MR MR

RUSSELIER, PETER
New York, N. Y.
1794

RUTTER, RICHARD
Baltimore, Md.
1790

Rutter Rutter

RYERSON, L.
York, Pa.
1760

L·Ryerson

S

SACKETT & WILLARD
Providence, R. I.
1815

SADD, HARVEY
New Hartford, Conn.
b. 1776, w. to 1829

H.SADD.

SADTLER, P. B. & SON
Baltimore, Md.
c. 1850

P.B.SADTLER&SON

SADTLER, PHILIP B.
Baltimore, Md.
1771-1860

P·S P.S P.S.
P.S PSadtler
P.S.

SADTLER & PFALTZ
Baltimore, Md.
c. 1800

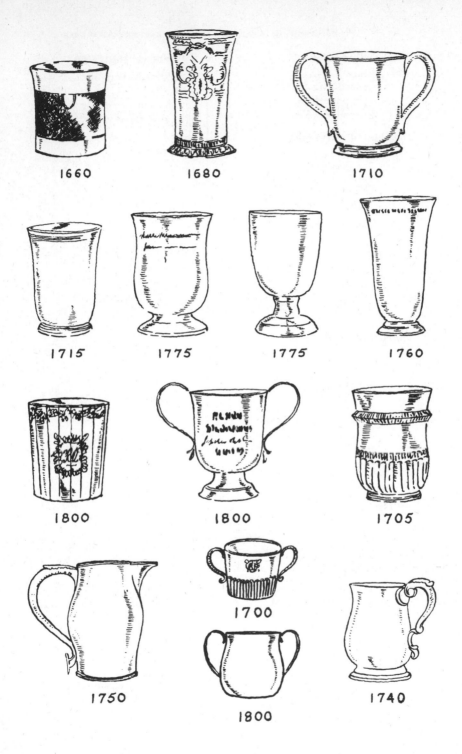

1660   1680   1710

1715   1775   1775   1760

1800   1800   1705

1750   1700   1740

1800

SAFFORD, HENRY
Ohio
w. 1800-1812

H.SAFFORD

SALISBURY, HENRY
New York, N. Y.
w.c. 1831-1838

SALISBURY N.Y.

SALISBURY & Co.

SANBORN, A.
Lowell, Mass.
c. 1850

A·SANBORN LOWELL

SANDELL, EDWARD
Baltimore, Md.
w. 1816, *d.* 1822

E·S

SANDERSON, BENJAMIN
Boston, Mass.
1649-1678

BS

SANDERSON, ROBERT
Boston, Mass.
1608-1693

RS RS RS

SANDERSON, WILLIAM
New York, N. Y.
1799

SANDFORD, F. S.
c. 1830

SANDOZ & BROTHER
New York, N. Y.
1811

SANDOZ, PHILIP A.
Philadelphia, Pa.
1814

SANDS, STEPHEN
New York, N. Y.
1774

SANFORD, FRED'K C.
Nantucket, Mass.
1809-1890, *w.* 1830-38

F.SANFORD

SANFORD, ISAAC
Hartford, Conn.
w. 1785-1793

SANFORD, WILLIAM
New York, N. Y.
1817

W SANFORD

SARDO, MICHAEL
Baltimore, Md.
1817

SARGEANT, ENSIGN
Boston, Mass.
1820

E.SARGEANT

SARGEANT, H.
Hartford, Conn.
c. 1825

H.Sargeant.

SARGEANT, JACOB (J) (W)
Hartford, Conn.
1761-1843

J·SARGEANT HART FORD

SARGEANT, THOMAS
Springfield, Mass.
c. 1810

T.SARGEANT

SARRAZIN, JONATHAN
Charleston, S. C.
18th Century

SARRAZIN, MOREAU
Charleston, S. C.
w. 1734-1761

MS

SAVAGE, EDWARD
Philadelphia, Pa.
1794

SAVAGE, JOHN Y.
Raleigh, N. C.
c. 1820

IYSAVAGE

SAVAGE & LYMAN

SAVAGE

LYMAN

SAVAGE, THOMAS
Boston, Mass.
1664-1749

TS   TS

SAVAGE, THOMAS, JR.
Boston, Mass.
1719

SAVAGE, W. M.
Glasgow, Ky.
1805

W.M.SAVAGE

SAWIN, SILAS W. (J)
New York, N. Y.
w. 1825-1838

SS   SS   SS

SAWYER, H. I.
New York, N. Y.
c. 1840

H.I.SAWYER

H.I.SAWYER

SAYRE, JOEL
New York, N. Y.
1778-1818

J.Sayre   I.SAYRE

J.SAYRE

SAYRE, JOHN
New York, N. Y.
1771-1852

SAYRE   JS

SAYRE, PAUL
Southampton, N. Y.
w. 1785

P.SAYRE

SAYRE & RICHARDS
New York, N. Y.
1802-1811

SCARRET, JOSEPH
Philadelphia, Pa.
1797

SCHAATS, BARTHOLOMEW
New York, N. Y.
1670-1758

SCHAATS, BARTHOLOMEW
New York, N. Y.
from 1784

SCHAFFIELD, JEREMIAH
Philadelphia, Pa.
1785

SCHANCK, GARRET
New York, N. Y.
w. 1791, d. 1795

GSCHANCK

SCHANCK, JOHN A.
New York, N. Y.
w. 1796

J.SCHANCK

SCHANCK

SCOFIELD, SALMON
Albany, N. Y., 1815
Rochester, N. Y., w. 1818-1827

SCHOOLFIELD
w. 1855

SCHOOLFIELD

SCOTT, I.
Albany, N. Y.
1750

I.SCOTT

SCOTT, JEHU
Raleigh, N. C.
w. 1806-1819

J.Scott

SCOTT, JOHN B.
New York, N. Y.
1820

SCOVIL & KINSEY
Cincinnati, Ohio
1830

SCOVILLKINSEY
CINCINNATI

SEAL, WILLIAM
Philadelphia, Pa.
c. 1817

W.SEAL

SEARS, MATTHEW
New York, N. Y.
1835

SEBASTIEN, JEANNE L.
New York, N. Y.
1814

SEGN, GEORGE
Philadelphia, Pa.
1820

SELKIRK, WILLIAM
New York, N. Y.
1817

SELL, J.
New York, N. Y.
1800

SEVEIGNES, JACQUES
New Orleans, La.
1822

SEVRIN, LEWIS
Philadelphia, Pa.
1837

SEXNINE, SIMON
New York, N. Y.
1722

SEYMOUR, H. P.

SEYMOUR & HOLLISTER
Hartford, Conn.
1845

SEYMOUR, JOSEPH
New York, N. Y.
1835

SEYMOUR, JOSEPH & CO.
Syracuse, N. Y.
late 19th Century

SEYMOUR, OLIVER D.
Hartford, Conn.
1843

SHARP, GEORGE
Philadelphia, Pa.
after 1850

SHARP, W.
Philadelphia, Pa.
1835

SHARP, W. & G.
Philadelphia, Pa.
1848

SHARPLEY, R.
w. 1855

SHARRARD, J. S.
Shelbyville, Ky.
1850

SHAVER, C. C.
Utica, N. Y.
after 1854

SHAW & DUNLEVY
Philadelphia, Pa.
1833

SHAW, EDWARD G.
Philadelphia, Pa.
1825

SHAW, JOHN A.
Newport, R. I.
1819

J·A·SHAW   J.SHAW

Pewter shovers

SHEPHERD & BOYD ✓
Albany, N. Y.
w. 1810-1830

S&B   SHEPHERD&BOYD

SHEPHERD, ROBERT
Albany, N. Y.
1805

SHEPHERD

R.Shepherd

SHEPPER, JOHN D.
Philadelphia, Pa.
1818

SHETHAR, SAMUEL
Litchfield, Conn.
c. 1800

SHETHAR & GORHAM
New Haven, Conn.
1806

SHETHAR & THOMPSON
Litchfield, Conn.
1801

S.&T.

SHIELDS, CALEB
Baltimore, Md.
1773

CS

SHIELDS, THOMAS
Philadelphia, Pa.
w. 1765-1791

T.S   TS

SHIPMAN, NATHANIEL
1764-1853

NS   N.SHIPMAN

SHIPP & COLLINS
Cincinnati, O.
c. 1850

SHIPP&COLLINS

SHIVING, GODFREY
Philadelphia, Pa.
1779

SHOEMAKER, CHARLES
New York, N. Y.
1825

SHOEMAKER, JOSEPH
Philadelphia, Pa.
w. 1798-1839

J.SHOEMAKER

Pitcher

SHONNARD, GEORGE
New York, N. Y.
1797

SHOPSHIRE, ROBERT
Baltimore, Md.
1778

SHREVE, BENJAMIN
Boston, Mass.
1834

beaker, maker unknown. Right: mug by
b Ten Eyck.

Helmet shape silver creamer. By
Joseph Shoemaker, Philadelphia.
Active 1793. $149.*

is van der Spiegel. Right: beaker by Benjamin Burt.

Left: cup with cover by Joseph Foster. Right: sugar bowl by John
Brevoort. (*All photos Courtesy of The Metropolitan Museum of Art*).

SIBLEY, ASA
Rochester, N. Y.
1764-1829

SIBLEY, CLARK
New Haven, Conn.
1778-1808

SIBLEY

SIBLEY, JAMES
Canandaigua, N. Y.
1779-1865

SIBLEY, JOHN
New Haven, Conn.
1810

J.SIBLEY

SIBLEY & MARBLE
New Haven, Conn.
w. 1801-1806

S&M

SILL, H.
New York, N. Y.
w. 1845-1850

H.SILL

SILL, H. & R. W. (J)
New York, N. Y.
w. 1840

H.& R.W. SILL

SILLIMAN, HEZEKIAH
New Haven, Conn.
1739-1804

HS

SIME & MOSES
Birmingham, Ga.
1768

SIME, WILLIAM
Birmingham, Ga.
1768

SIMES, WILLIAM
Portsmouth, N. H.
1773-1824

W.S   W.SIMES
W.SIMES

SIMMONS & ALEXANDER
Philadelphia, Pa.
w. 1798-1804

SIMMONS&
ALEXANDER   S&A

SIMMONS, ANTHONY
Philadelphia, Pa.
w. 1796-1808

A.S   A.S   A.SIMMONS
A.SIMMONS

SIMMONS, J. & A.
New York, N. Y.
w. 1805-1813

J.&A.S.   J.&ASIMMONS

SIMMONS, JAMES
New York, N. Y.
c. 1815

J.Simmons

SIMMONS, JOSEPH
Philadelphia, Pa.
1828

SIMMONS, PETER
New York, N. Y.
1816

SIMMONS, S.
Philadelphia, Pa.
1797

[S.SIMMONS]

SIMMONS & WILLIAMSON
Philadelphia, Pa.
1797

[S&W]

SIMPKINS, THOMAS B.
Boston, Mass.
1728-1804

[T.B.Simpkins]

[T.SIMPKINS]

SIMPKINS, WILLIAM
Boston, Mass.
1704-1780

[WS] [WS] [Simpkins]

[W.SIMPKINS]

[W.Simpkins]

[WSIMPKINS]

SIMPSON & BECKEL
Albany, N. Y.
1849

SINGLETON & YOUNG
New York, N. Y.
1800

SIXTE, JOSEPH ·A.
Philadelphia, Pa.
1837

SIXTE, VINCENT B.
Philadelphia, Pa.
1837

SKERRET, JOSEPH
Philadelphia, Pa.
1797

SKERRY, GEORGE W.
Boston, Mass.
1837

SKINNER, ABRAHAM
New York, N. Y.
1756

[A.Skinner]

[Skinner]

SKINNER, ELIZER
Hartford, Conn.
w. 1826, d. 1858

SKINNER, MATT
Philadelphia, Pa.
1752

[MATT SKINNER]

SKINNER, THOMAS
Marblehead, Mass.
1712-1761

[TS] _

SLIDELL, JOSHUA
New York, N. Y.
1765

[SLIDELL] [NYORK]

SLOAN, WILLIAM
Hartford, Conn.
1794

SMITH, DAVID
Philadelphia, Pa.
w. 1778-1793

[D.SMITH]

SMITH, CHRISTIAN
Philadelphia, Pa.
1820

SMITH, EBENEZER
Brookfield, Conn.
w.c. 1790

SMITH, FLOYD (Retailer)
New York, N. Y.
1815-1836

FLOYD SMITH

SMITH, GEORGE
Philadelphia, Pa.
1831

SMITH, GEORGE O.
New York, N. Y.
1825

SMITH & GRANT
Louisville, Ky.
c. 1830

Smith & Grant

SMITH, JACOB
Philadelphia, Pa.
1809

SMITH, JAMES
New York, N. Y.
1794

SMITH, JAMES
Philadelphia, Pa.
1807

SMITH, JOHN
Baltimore, Md.
1814

I·SMITH

SMITH, JOHN L.
Syracuse, N. Y.
c. 1850

J.L.SMITH

SMITH, JOHN & THOMAS
Baltimore, Md.
1817

SMITH, JOSEPH
Boston, Mass.
1742-1789

IS   I·SMITH

SMITH, JOSEPH
Philadelphia, Pa.
1804

SMITH, J. & T.
Baltimore, Md.
1817

SMITH, LEVIN H.
Philadelphia, Pa.
1837

SMITH, RICHARD E.
Louisville, Ky.
1827

RESMITH

SMITH, SAMUEL
Philadelphia, Pa.
1785

SMITH, WILLIAM
New York, N. Y.
1770

SMITH, WILLIAM (W)
New York, N. Y.
w. 1817-1840

Wm SMITH

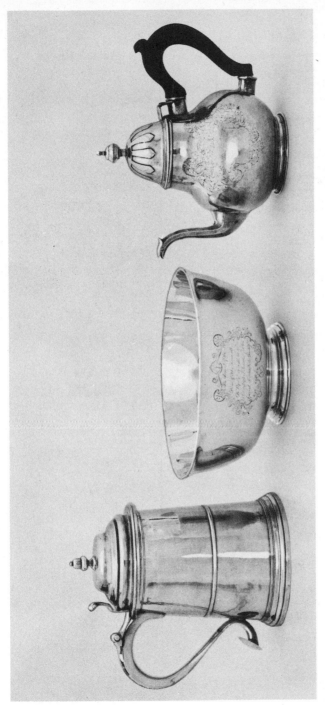

Left to right: tankard by Benjamin Burt; bowl by Adrian Bancker; teapot by Peter Van Dyke. (*Courtesy of The Metropolitan Museum of Art*).

SMITH, ZEBULON
Maine
1786-1865

SNOW, JEREMIAH
Williamsburg, Mass.
c. 1810

SNYDER, GEORGE
Philadelphia, Pa.
1816

SOLOMON, SAMUEL
Philadelphia, Pa.
1811

SOMERBY, ROBERT
Massachusetts
1794-1821

SONNIER, JOSEPH
Philadelphia, Pa.
1811

SOQUE, MICHAEL
New York, N. Y.
1794

SOUMAINE, SAMUEL
Philadelphia, Pa.
1718-1765

SOUMAINE, SIMEON
New York, N. Y.
1685-1750

SOWERLT, ANTHONY
Philadelphia, Pa.
1823

SPARROW, HENRY
Philadelphia, Pa.
1811

SPARROW, THOMAS
Annapolis, Md.
w. 1764-1784

SPEAR, ISAAC
Boston, Mass.
1836

SPEAR, JAMES E.
Charleston, S. C.
c. 1846-1871

SPEER, ISAAC (W)
Newark, N. J.
c. 1837

SPENCE, G.
Newark, N. J.
w.c. 1830-1840

G. SPENCE
NEWARK, N. J.

SPENCER, GEORGE
Essex, Conn.
1787-1878

SPENCER, JAMES
Hartford, Conn.
1793

SPENCER, JAMES JR.
Hartford, Conn.
w. 1843

SQUIRE & BROTHER
New York, N. Y.
1846

[SQUIRE & BROTHER of COIN]

SQUIRE & LANDER
New York, N. Y.
1840

SQUIRE & LANDER

SQUIRE, S. P.
New York, N. Y.
1835

[S.P.SQUIRE]

STACY, PHILEMON
Boston, Mass.
1819

[P.STACY]

STALL, JOSEPH
Baltimore, Md.
1804

STANIFORD, JOHN
Windham, Conn.
1737-1811

[JS] [Staniford]

STANTON, DANIEL
Stonington, Conn.
1755-1781

[D.Stanton]

STANTON, D., E., & Z.
Stonington, Conn.
c. 1775-1780

STANTON, ENOCH
Stonington, Conn.
1745-1781

[E.S]

STANTON, WILLIAM P. (W) (J)
Hudson, N. Y., 1801
Nantucket, Mass.
w. 1821

STANTON, W. P. & H.
Rochester, N. Y.
1826-1841

[W.P. & H. STANTON]

STANTON, ZEBULON
Stonington, Conn.
1753-1828

[ZS] [STANTON]

STANWOOD & HALSTRICK
Boston, Mass.
1850

STANWOOD, HENRY B.
Boston, Mass.
1818-1869

[Henry B. Stanwood]

STANWOOD, J. E.
Philadelphia, Pa.
1850

[JE STANWOOD]

STANWOOD, JAMES D.
Boston, Mass.
1846

STAPLES, JOHN J. JR.
New York, N. Y.
1788

 (IIS) [J.J.S.]

ST. CYR, S. L.
New Orleans, La.
1822

STARR, JASPER
New London, Conn.
1709-1792

STARR, RICHARD
Philadelphia, Pa.
c. 1810

[RSTARR]   [R·STARR]

STEBBINS, T. E. & CO.
New York, N. Y.
c. 1835

[E.STEBBINS✓CO]

STEBBINS & HOWE
New York, N. Y.
1832

[STEBBINS & HOWE]

STEBBINS, THOMAS E. (W)
New York, N. Y.
w. 1828-1833

[STEBBINS]   [T.STEBBINS]

STEDMAN, ALEXANDER
Philadelphia, Pa.
1793

STEELE, JAMES P.
Rochester, N. Y.
1811-1893

[JAS.P.STEELE]

STEELE, JOHN
Annapolis, Md.
1710

STEELE, T. & CO.
Hartford, Conn.
c. 1815

[T.Steele & Co]

STEELE, T. S.
Hartford, Conn.
c. 1800

[T.Steele]

STEPHEN, THOMAS H.
Philadelphia, Pa.
1839

STEPHENS, GEORGE
New York, N. Y.
c. 1790

[G.S]

STEPHENSON, THOMAS
Buffalo, N. Y.
w. 1835-1848

STEPHENSON

STEVEN, GEORGE
New York, N. Y.
1719

STEVENS & LAKEMAN
Salem, Mass.
1819-1830

[STEVENS &LAKEMAN]

STEWART
c. 1830

[STEWART]   [IO.IS]

STEWART, C. W.
Lexington, Ky.
1850

C.W.STEWART LEX.KT.

1660

1700

1725

1775

1795

1775

1740

1700

1700

STEWART, JOHN
New York, N. Y.
1791
STEWART IO·IS

STICKLER, JOHN
New York, N. Y.
1823

STICKNEY, JONATHAN
Newburyport, Mass.
1798
J·STICKNEY

STICKNEY, M. P.
Newburyport, Mass.
1820
M.P.STICKNEY

STILES & BALDWIN
Northampton, Mass.
1791

STILES, BENJAMIN
Woodbury, Conn.
1831

STILLMAN, ALEXANDER
Philadelphia, Pa.
1806

STILLMAN, BARTON
Westerly, R. I.

STILLMAN, E.
Stonington, Conn.
1825
E. Stillman E.Stillman

STILLMAN, PAUL
Westerly, R. I.

STILLMAN, RICHARD
Philadelphia, Pa.
1805
R.STILLMAN

STILLMAN, SAMUEL S.
Hartford, Conn.
w. 1850

STILLMAN, WILLIAM
Hopkington, R. I.
1788

STINSON, WILLIAM
New York, N. Y.
1813

STOCKMAN & PEPPER
Philadelphia, Pa.
c. 1840
STOCKMAN & PEPPER

STOCKMAN, JACOB
Philadelphia, Pa.
w. 1828-1850
J. STOCKMAN

STODDER & FROBISHER
Boston, Mass.
1817-1825
STODDER & FROBISHER

STODDER, JONATHAN (J)
New York, N. Y.
c. 1828
J. STODDER

STOLLENWERCK & BROS.
New York, N. Y.
1805
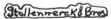
Stollenwerck & Bros

STOLLENWERCK & CO.
New York, N. Y.
1800

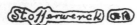

STONE, ADAM
Baltimore, Md.
w. 1804

AS

STONE & OSBORN
New York, N. Y.
1796

STORM, ABRAHAM G.
Albany, N. Y.
1779-1836

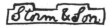

STORM, A. G. & SON
Albany, N. Y.
c. 1825

Storm & Son.

STORM, E. C.
Rochester, N. Y.
1815

E.C.STORM

STORM & WILSON
Poughkeepsie, N. Y.
1802-1818

S. & WILSON

STORRS & COOK
Northampton, Mass.
c. 1830

Storrs & Cook

STORRS & COOLEY
Utica, N. Y.
1831-1839

 Storrs & Cooley. S & C

STORRS, NATHAN
Northampton, Mass.
1768-1839

N. STORRS

STORY, S. N.
Worcester, Mass.
mid 19th Century

 S.N.Story WORCESTER

STOUT, JAMES D.
New York, N. Y.
w. 1817-1836

  JDSTOUT

STOUT, SAMUEL
Princeton, N. J.
1780

STOUTENBURGH, LUKE
Charleston, S. C.
w.c. 1718-1743

 LSB S V B

STOUTENBURGH, TOBIAS
New York, N. Y.
1700-1759

TSB TSB

STOW, JOHN P.
Wilmington, Del.
1748-1802

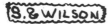

STOWELL, A.
Baltimore, Md.
1855

A STOWELL JR

STRIKER, GEORGE W. (W)
New York, N. Y.
w. 1825-1835

G.W.STRIKER

STRONG, JOHN
Maryland
1778

STRONG, WILLIAM
Philadelphia, Pa.
1807

STUART, H.
New York, N. Y.
1808

STUART, JOHN (J)
Providence, R. I.
d. 1737

IS Stuart ✷Stuart✷

STUCKERT, ISAAC
Philadelphia, Pa.
1809

STUDLEY, D. F.
c. 1830

D.F.STUDLEY.

SULLIVAN, C. D.
St. Louis, Mo.
c. 1850

CDSULLIVAN

SULLIVAN, D. & CO.
New York, N. Y.
1820

D.SULLIVAN & Co

SUPPLEE, JACOB
Philadelphia, Pa.
1791

SUTHERLAND, GEORGE
Boston, Mass.
1810

SUTTON, ROBERT
New Haven, Conn.
1815

SWAN, B.
c. 1825

B.SWAN

SWAN, CALEB
Boston, Mass.
1775

SWAN, ROBERT
Andover, Mass., *w.* 1795
Philadelphia, Pa., *w.* 1799-1831

R SWAN R.SWAN
R.SWAN

SWAN, WILLIAM
Worcester, Mass.
1715-1774

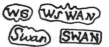
WS WS WAN
Swan SWAN

Reading down, marks of the following silversmiths: 1-3, Paul Revere; 4. Peter Van Dyke; 5. William Cowell; 6. Paul Revere (with monogram of owners) ; 7. Benjamin Burt. (*Courtesy of The Metropolitan Museum of Art*).

SWEENEY, JOHN
Geneva, N. Y.
w. 1816-1827

SWEETER, HENRY P.
Worcester, Mass.
1768

SYMMES, JOHN
Boston, Mass.
1767

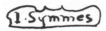

SYNG, DANIEL
Lancaster, Pa.
w. 1713-1734

SYNG, JOHN
Philadelphia, Pa.
w. 1734

SYNG, PHILIP
Philadelphia, Pa.
1676-1739

SYNG, PHILIP, JR.
Philadelphia, Pa.
1703-1789

T

TABER, S. M. & CO.

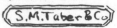

TABER, WILLIAM
Philadelphia, Pa.
1835

TAFT, R.
R.TAFT

TANGUY, J. & P.
Philadelphia, Pa.
1808

TANGUY, JOHN
Philadelphia, Pa.
w. 1801-1822

TANGUY, PETER
Philadelphia, Pa.
1810

TANNER, JOHN
Newport, R. I.
1713-1785

TANNER, PERRY G.
Cooperstown, N. Y.
w. 1842-1850

PG TANNER

TANNER & ROGERS
  Newport, R. I.
  1750

  T&R

TARBELL, E.
  c. 1830

TARGEE, JOHN
  New York, N. Y.
  w.c. 1800-1815

TARGEE, JOHN & PETER
  New York, N. Y.
  w. 1811

  J*PT   I*P.TARGEE

TARGEE, PETER
  New York, N. Y.
  1811

TARGEE, WILLIAM
  New York, N. Y.
  1807

TAYLOR, GEORGE W.
  Philadelphia, Pa.
  1824

TAYLOR & HINSDALE (J)
  New York, N. Y.
  w. 1817-1829

  T&H

TAYLOR, JOHN
  New York, N. Y.
  1801

TAYLOR & LAWRIE
  Philadelphia, Pa.
  1841

TAYLOR & LAWRIE
  Philadelphia, Pa.
  1837

  TAYLOR&LAWRIE

TAYLOR, NAJAH
  New York, N. Y.
  1793

TAYLOR, N. & CO.
  New York, N. Y.
  1825

  N TAYLOR & CO

TAYLOR, THOMAS
  Providence, R. I.
  1727

TAYLOR, WILLIAM
  Philadelphia, Pa.
  c. 1775

  W.T

TEMPEST, ROBERT
  Philadelphia, Pa.
  1814

TEN EYCK, BARENT
  Albany, N. Y.
  1714-1795

  B·E

TEN EYCK, JACOB
  Albany, N. Y.
  1704-1793

TEN EYCK, KOENRAET
New York, N. Y.
1678-1753

[KE] [KE]

TENNEY, WILLIAM I. (J)
New York, N. Y.
w. 1830-1850

[I.TENNEY] [261 B.WAY]

TERRY, GEER
Worcester, Mass.
Enfield, Conn.
1775-1858

[G.TERRY] [TERRY]

TERRY, JOHN
New York, N. Y.
1820

TERRY, L. B.
Enfield, Conn.
w. 1810

[L.B.TERRY]

TERRY, WILBERT
Enfield, Conn.
w. 1780-1810

[W.TERRY]

THAXTER, JOSEPH B.
Hingham, Mass.
1791-1863

[J.B.THAXTER]

THEOFILE, WILLIAM
New Orleans, La.
1822

THIBAULT & BROS.
Philadelphia, Pa.
1810

[THIBAULT BROTHERS]

THIBAULT & CO.
Philadelphia, Pa.
1797

THIBAULT, FELIX (J)
Philadelphia, Pa.
1814

THIBAULT, FRANCIS (J)
Philadelphia, Pa.
1800

THIBAULT, FRANCIS & FELIX (J)
Philadelphia, Pa.
1807

[F&F.THIBAULT]

[.THIBAULT]

THIBAULT, FREDERICK
Philadelphia, Pa.
1818

THIBAULT, FRED'K & FELIX
Philadelphia, Pa.
1813

THOMAS, CARSON & HALL
Albany, N. Y.
1818

[T.C&H]

THOMAS, THOMAS
New York, N. Y.
1784

THOMAS, WALTER
New York, N. Y.
1769

[W.T]

THOMAS, WILLIAM
Trenton, N. J.
1775

THOMISON, PETER
Boston, Mass.
1817

THOMPSON, D. B.
Litchfield, Conn.
1825

[D.B.Thomson .]

THOMPSON, I.

[I·THOMPSON]

THOMPSON, WILLIAM
Baltimore, Md.
w. 1795-1021

[WT]

THOMSON, F.

[F.THOMSON]

THOMSON, ISAAC
Litchfield, Conn.
w. 1801-1805

[I.THOMSON]

THOMSON, JAMES
New York, N. Y.
w. 1834-1840

[Jas.Thomson]

THOMSON, PETER
Philadelphia, Pa.
1835

THOMSON, WILLIAM
New York, N. Y.
w. 1815-1834

[Wm.Thomson]

[W.Thomson]

THORNTON, HENRY
Providence, R. I.
1824

TILEY, JAMES
Hartford, Conn.
1740-1792

[I·TILEY] [Tiley]

TINGLEY, SAMUEL
New York, N. Y.
w.c. 1765-1790

[S.T Tingley] [N.York]

TINKHAM, F. & CO. (W)
New York, N. Y.
w. 1840

[F.TINKHAM & C?]

TISDALE, B. H.
Providence, R. I.
c. 1824

[BHTISDALE]

[BH.Tisdale]

TITCOMB, FRANCIS
Newburyport, Mass.
1790-1832
F.TITCOMB

TITUS, JAMES (W)
Philadelphia, Pa.
1833
I.TITUS   STANDARD

TOMPKINS, EDMUND
Waterbury, Conn.
b. 1757, w. 1779

TOUZELL, JOHN
Salem, Mass.
1726-1785
IT J.TOUZELL
J Touzell

TOWN, IRA S.
Montpelier, Vt.
1825
IRA S.TOWN

TOWNSHENDT, THOMAS
Boston, Mass.
1701-1777

TOWNSEND, S.
1775
S.TOWNSEND
ST Townsend

TOWSON, OBADIAH W.
Philadelphia, Pa.
1819
 O.W.TOWSON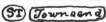

TOY, ISAAC NICHOLAS
Maryland
1771-1834
I.N.TOY

TOY, JOSEPH
Abingdon, Md.
1748-1826
I.T. I.T.

TOY & WILSON
Abingdon, Md.
1790
I.T. W.W.

TOZER, JUNIUS F.
Rochester, N. Y.
c. 1850

TRACY, ERASTUS
Norwich, Conn.
1768-1795

TRACY, GORDON
Norwich, Conn.
1767-1792
G.TRACY

TREZEVANT, DANIEL
Charleston, S. C.

TRIPLER, CHRISTIAN
New York, N. Y.
1794

TROLL, WILLIAM
Philadelphia, Pa.
1810

TROTH, JAMES
Pittsburgh, Pa.
1800

Snuffer stand and snuffers by Cornelius Kierstede. (*Courtesy of The Metropolitan Museum of Art*).

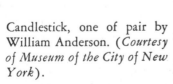

Candlestick, one of pair by William Anderson. (*Courtesy of Museum of the City of New York*).

TROTT & BROOKS
New London, Conn.
1798

T&B

TROTT & CLEVELAND
New London, Conn.
1792-1794

T&C

TROTT, GEORGE
Boston, Mass.
1765

TROTT, J. P. & SON
New London, Conn.
1820

JPT&Son   I-PT&SON

IPT&SON

TROTT, JOHN P.
New London, Conn.
1769-1852

JPT   J·P·T   JPT

J·P·TROTT

TROTT, JONATHAN
Boston, Mass.
1730-1815

J·TROTT   I·TROTT

TROTT, JONATHAN, JR.
New London, Conn.
1771-1813

I·T

TROTT, THOMAS
Boston, Mass.
1701-1777

TT

TRUAX, HENRY R.
Albany, N. Y.
1760-1834

HRT

H.R.T

TRUMBULL, RICHARD
Boston, Mass.
1767

TUCKER, DANIEL
Portland, Me.
1781

TUCKER, J. W.
New York, N. Y.
1803

TURNER, FRANKLIN
Cheraw, S. C.
c. 1812

TURNER, JAMES
Boston, Mass.
d. 1759

IT

TUTHILL, CHRISTOPHER
Philadelphia, Pa.
1731

TUTTLE, BETHUEL
New Haven, Conn.
1779-1813

TUTTLE, WILLIAM
New Haven, Conn.
1800-1849

TWEDY & BARROWS

TYLER, ANDREW

Boston, Mass.

1692-1741

TYLER, DAVID

Boston, Mass.

1760-1804

TYLER, D. M.

Boston, Mass.

1810

TYLER, GEORGE

Boston, Mass.

1740-1785

TYLER, JOHN H. & CO.

Boston, Mass.

1840

TYRREL, A. B.

U

UBELIN, FREDERICK

Philadelphia, Pa.

1773

UFFORD & BURDICK

New Haven, Conn.

c. 1810

UNDERHILL, ANDREW

New York, N. Y.

w. 1780

UNDERHILL, THOMAS

New York, N. Y.

w. 1787

UNDERHILL & VERNON

New York, N. Y.

1787

UNDERWOOD, JOHN

Philadelphia, Pa.

1797

V

VAIL, ELIJAH

Troy, N. Y.

1836

VAISSIERE, VICTOR

New York, N. Y.

1816

VALET, PETER

New York, N. Y.

1787

VALLEE, ANTOINE
New Orleans, La.
1822

VALLANT, WILLIAM
Philadelphia, Pa.
w. 1752

VANALL, JOHN
Charleston, S. C.
w.c. 1749-c. 1767

VAN BERGEN, JOHN
Albany, N. Y.
1813

VAN BEUREN, PETER
New York, N. Y.
w. 1795

VAN BEUREN, WILLIAM
New York, N. Y.
w. 1794

VANDERBURGH, CORNELIUS
New York, N. Y.
1652-1699

VAN DER SPIEGEL, JACOBUS
New York, N. Y.
1668-1708

VAN DYKE, PETER
New York, N. Y.
1684-1751

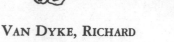

VAN DYKE, RICHARD
New York, N. Y.
1717-1770

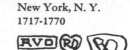

VAN HORN, DAVID
Philadelphia, Pa.
1801

VAN INBURGH, PETER
New York, N. Y.
1689-1740

VAN NESS & WATERMAN
New York, N. Y.
1835

VAN RENSSELAER, NICHOLAS
Albany, N. Y.
c. 1765

VAN RIPER, TUNIS
New York, N. Y.
w. 1815-1829

VANSANT & CO.
Philadelphia, Pa.
c. 1880

Tankard by William Vilant. (*Courtesy of Philadelphia Museum of Art*).

Left: sugar bowl by Littleton Holland. (*Courtesy of Philadelphia Museum of Art*). Right: teapot by John A. Schanck. (*Courtesy of The Metropolitan Museum of Art*).

VAN SCHAICK, G.
Albany, N. Y.
1840

VAN STEENBERG, JOHN
Kingston, N. Y.
c. 1775

VAN VEGHTEN, HENRY
Albany, N. Y.
1760

VAN VLEIT, B.
Poughkeepsie, N. Y.
1840

B.VANVLEIT.

VAN VOORHIS, DANIEL
Philadelphia, Pa.
New York, N. Y.
1751-1824

VAN VOORHIS & COLEY
New York, N. Y.
1786

VAN VOORHIS & SCHANCK
New York, N. Y.
1791

VAN VOORHIS, SCHANCK
& MCCALL
Albany, N. Y.
c. 1800

VAN VOORHIS & SON
New York, N. Y.
1798

VAN WYCK & PELLETREAU
New York, N. Y.
1815

VAN WYCK, STEPHEN
New York, N. Y.
1810

SVANWYCK

VARNEY, JOHN
Philadelphia, Pa.
1795

VEAL & GLAZE
Columbia, S. C.
1838-c. 1841

VEAL, JOHN
Columbia, S. C.
w.c. 1826-1857

VEAZIE, JOSEPH
Providence, R. I.
1815

VERGEREAU, PETER
New York, N. Y.
1700-1755

VERNON, J. & CO.
New York, N. Y.
1798

VERNON, JOHN
New York, N. Y.
w. 1768-1815

VERNON, NATHANIEL
Charleston, S. C.
1777-1843

VERNON, NATHANIEL & CO.
Charleston, S. C.
1802-1808

VERNON & PARK
Pittsburgh, Pa.
1815

VERNON, SAMUEL
Newport, R. I.
1683-1737

VILANT, WILLIAM
Philadelphia, Pa.
w. 1725

VILLARD, R. H. L.
Washington, D. C.
1833

VINCENT, RICHARD
Baltimore, Md.
1799

VINTON, DAVID
Providence, R. I.
1790

VIRGIN, W. M.
1830

VOGLER, JOHN
Salem, N. C.
1783-1881

VOORHEES, A.

W

WACHNER, F. W.
New York, N. Y.
1819

WADDILL, NOEL
Petersburg, Va.
1778

WAGLIN, THOMAS
Philadelphia, Pa.
1837

WAGSTAFF, THOMAS
New York, N. Y.
1791

WAGSTER, ISAIAH
Baltimore, Md.
w. 1776-1793

WAIT & WRIGHT
Philadelphia, Pa.
1837

WAITE, JOHN
Kingston, R. I.
c. 1770

WAITE, WILLIAM
Wickford, R. I.
1760

WAKEFIELD & WOODWARD
Great Falls, N. H.

WALDRON, D.
New York, N. Y.
1789

WALKER, GEORGE
Philadelphia, Pa.
1797

WALKER, HANNAH
Philadelphia, Pa.
1816

WALKER, JOHN
Philadelphia, Pa.
1798

WALKER, L.
Boston, Mass.
1825

WALKER, WILLIAM
Philadelphia, Pa.
w. 1793-1816

WALKER, W. & S.
Philadelphia, Pa.
1795

WALLACE, WILLIAM F.
Westerly, R. I.

WALLEN, JOHN
Philadelphia, Pa.
1763

WALLIS, THOMAS
Philadelphia, Pa.
1804

WALRAVEN, JOHN
Baltimore, Md.
1771-1814

WALTER, JACOB
Baltimore, Md.
1782-1865

Top: porringer, late 18th century, maker unknown.
Bottom; inkstand by John Coney. (*Courtesy of
The Metropolitan Museum of Art*).

WALTER, JOSEPH M.
Baltimore, Md.
1835

JOS.M.WALTER. 10.02.15.

WALTON, DANIEL
Philadelphia, Pa.
1808

WALWORTH, DANIEL
Middletown, Conn.
1760-1830

WARD, AMBROSE
New Haven, Conn.
1735-1808

AW

WARD & BARTHOLOMEW
Hartford, Conn.
w. 1804-1809

W&B W&B
WARD & BARTHOL OMEW. HARTFORD
WARD& BARTHOLOMEW HARTFORD

WARD, BARTHOLOMEW &
BRAINARD
Hartford, Conn.
1809-1830

WARD, BILIOUS
Guilford, Conn.
1729-1777

BW BW BW B.W

WARD & COX
Hartford, Conn.
1811

WARD & GAVETT
Hartford, Conn.
1813

WARD & HUGHES
Middletown, Conn.
1805

WARD, JAMES
Hartford, Conn.
1768-1856

JW WARD HARTFORD

WARD, J. & W. L. (W)
Philadelphia, Pa.
w. 1837-1850

JEHU & W.L. WARD PHILA

WARD, JOHN
Middletown, Conn.
1805

WARD.67 MARKET ST.

WARD & MILLER
Philadelphia, Pa.
1822

WARD & RICH
Boston, Mass.
1830

WARD, RICHARD
Boston, Mass.
1815

WARD, SAMUEL L.
Boston, Mass.
1830

WARD, TIMOTHY
Middletown, Conn.
1742-1768

WARD, WILLIAM
Guilford, Conn.
1705-1761

WARD, WILLIAM
Litchfield, Conn.
1736-1826

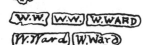

WARDEN, ABIJAH B. (J)
Philadelphia, Pa.
w. 1842-1850

WARDEN

WARDIN, DANIEL
Bridgeport, Conn.
1811

WARFORD, JOSEPH
Albany, N. Y.
1810

WARFORD

WARNER, A. E. & T. H.
Baltimore, Md.
1805

T.& A.E.WARNER

WARNER, ANDREW E. (W)
Baltimore, Md.
1786-1870

A.E.W   A.E.W

A.E.W   A.E.WARNER

ANDW E.WARNER

A.E.WARNER

WARNER, CALEB
Salem, Mass.
1784-1861

C.Warner

C.Warner   C.WARNER

WARNER, C. & J.
Baltimore, Md.
1825

C.&J.WARNER

WARNER, D.
Ipswich, Mass.
1820

D.WARNER

WARNER & FELLOWS
Portsmouth, N. H.
1824

WARNER, JOSEPH
Wilmington, Del.
w. 1768-1792

J.Warner

WARNER, JOSEPH P.
Baltimore, Md.
1811-1862

J.P.W

WARNER, SAMUEL
Philadelphia, Pa.
w. 1797-1812
⬚ S·W ⬚ ⬚ WARNER ⬚

WARNER, THOMAS & A. E.
Baltimore, Md.
1805
⬚ T·&·A·E·WARNER ⬚

WARNER, THOMAS H.
Baltimore, Md.
1780-1828
⬚ T.W ⬚ ⬚ T.WARNER ⬚ ⬚ T ⬚

WARREN, BENJAMIN
Philadelphia, Pa.
1809

WATERMAN, GEORGE
Albany, N. Y.
1849

WATERS, SAMUEL
Boston, Mass.
c. 1790
⬚ S·W ⬚ ⬚ SW ⬚ ⬚ S·WATERS ⬚

WATKINS, JAMES
New York, N. Y.
1819

WATKINS, JAMES
Philadelphia, Pa.
1837

WATSON & BROWN
Philadelphia, Pa.
1830
⬚ WATSON & BROWN ⬚

WATSON, EDWARD (J)
Boston, Mass.
w. 1821, *d.* 1839
⬚ E.WATSON ⬚ ⬚ E.Watson ⬚

WATSON, JAMES
Philadelphia, Pa.
1830
⬚ J WATSON ⬚

WATTS, J. & W.
Philadelphia, Pa.
1829

WATTS, JAMES
Philadelphia, Pa.
1835

WATTS, JOHN W.
New York, N. Y.
1794

WAYNES, RICHARD
Philadelphia, Pa.
1750

WEATHERS, MICHAEL
New York, N. Y.
1794

WEAVER, EMMOR T.
Philadelphia, Pa.
w. 1808-1820

WEAVER, JOSHUA
West Chester, Pa.
c. 1815

Left: caddy by Abraham Carlisle. Right: teapot by J. and N. Richardson. (*Courtesy Philadelphia Museum of Art*).

WEAVER, NICHOLAS N.
Utica, N. Y.
1791-1853

N.N.WEAVER.

WEBB, BARNABAS
Boston, Mass.
w. 1756-1789

BW   B.W

WEBB & BOON
Philadelphia, Pa.
1785

WEBB, CHARLES
Philadelphia, Pa.
1738

WEBB, EDWARD
Boston, Mass.
d. 1718

WEBB   EW

WEBB, GEORGE W.
Baltimore, Md.
1812-1890

GWWEBB   TD 13

GEO.W.WEBB

WEBB, JAMES
Baltimore, Md.
1788-1844

J.WEBB B

WEBB, ROBERT
Philadelphia, Pa.
1798

WEBSTER, HENRY L.
Providence, R. I.
1831

H.L.WEBSTER

WEBSTER, HENRY L. & CO.
Providence, R. I.
1842

H.L.Webster & Co.

H.L.W & CO Providence RI

WEDGE, SIMON
Baltimore, Md.
1774-1823

S.Wedge S.WEDGE

S.W   SW

WEEDEN, PELEG
N. Kingston, R. I.
w. 1803

WELCH, JOHN
Boston, Mass.

WELLES, A. & G.
Boston, Mass.
c. 1807

A*G.WELLES

WELLES, ALFRED
Hebron, Conn.
1783-1860

Wa   WELLES X

WELLES & CO.
Boston, Mass.
1816-1821

WELLES&CO

WELLES & GELSTON
New York, N. Y.
1840

WELLES, GEORGE
Boston, Mass.
1784-1823

WELLES, JAMES M.
New York, N. Y.
1835

WELLS, L. & C.
New York, N. Y.
1798

WELLS, L. & H.
New York, N. Y.
1794

WELLS, LEMUEL
New York, N. Y.
1791

WELLS, LEMUEL & CO.
New York, N. Y.
1794

WELLS, WILLIAM
Hartford, Conn.
b. 1766

WENDOVER, JOHN
New York, N. Y.
w. 1694, d. 1727

WENMAN, BERNARD
New York, N. Y.
w. 1796-1834

WENTWORTH, JASON
Boston, Mass.
1846

WENTWORTH & CO.
New York, N. Y.
1850

WESCOAT, I.

WEST, B.
Boston, Mass.
c. 1830

WEST, CHARLES
Boston, Mass.
1830

WEST, JOSEPH
Philadelphia, Pa.
1797

WESTERMEYER, HENRY
Charleston, S. C.
c. 1790

WESTERVELT, JOHN L.
Newburgh, N. Y.
1845

J.LW

WESTON, BENJAMIN
Philadelphia, Pa.
1797

WESTPHAL, CHARLES W.
Philadelphia, Pa.
1802

C.WESTPHAL

C.WESTPHAL

WHARTENBY & BUNN
Philadelphia, Pa.
1816

WHARTENBY, JOHN
Philadelphia, Pa.
1829

WHARTENBY, THOMAS
Philadelphia, Pa.
1811

T.W   WHARTENBY

WHARTENBY, THOMAS, & CO.
Philadelphia, Pa.
c. 1850

WHEATLEY, FRED'K G.
New York, N. Y.
1805

WHEATON, CALVIN
Providence, R. I.
1791

C WHEATON

C WHEATON

WHEELER, I.

J Wheeler

WHEELER & BROOKS
Livonia, N. Y.
c. 1830

WHEELERS & BROOKS

WHETCROFT, WILLIAM
Baltimore, Md.
1735-1799

WW

WHIPPLE, ARNOLD
Providence, R. I.
1825

WHITAKER & GREEN
Providence, R. I.
1825

WHITE, ALFRED
Boston, Mass.
1807

WHITE, AMOS
E. Haddam, Conn.
1745-1825

A.WHITE   WHITE

WHITE, C.
Mobile, Ala.
c. 1830-40

C.WHITE MOBILE

WHITE, EDWARD
Ulster County, N. Y.
1757

E:WHITE

18th Century American silver including pieces by John Coney, Timothy Dwight, John Edwards, Peter Oliver, and John Coburn. (*Courtesy Museum of Fine Arts, Boston*).

WHITE, GEORGE L.
Cincinnati, Ohio
1822

WHITE, PEREGRINE
Woodstock, Conn.
1747-1834

P.WHITE

WHITE, PETER
Norwalk, Conn.
1718-1803

WHITE, S. & CO.
New York, N. Y.
c. 1830

S.WHITE & CO

WHITE, SAMUEL
New York, N. Y.
1805

WHITE, SILAS
New York, N. Y.
1754-1798

S.WHITE

WHITE, STEPHEN
New York, N. Y.
1805

WHITE, WILLIAM
Philadelphia, Pa.
1805

WHITE, WILLIAM J.
New York, N. Y.
1835

WHITE, WILLIAM W.
New York, N. Y.
w. 1827-1841

WWWHITE

W: W WHITE

WHITEMAN, IRA
New York, N. Y.
1761

WHITING, B.
Norwich, Conn.
1755

B: WHITING

WHITING, CHARLES
Norwich, Conn.
1725-1765

CW WHITING

WHITING, S.
New York, N. Y.
c. 1700

WHITLOCK, THOMAS
New York, N. Y.
w. 1796-1805

Whitlock

WHITLOCK, WILLIAM H. (W.)
New York, N. Y.
w. 1805-1827

WHH.WHITLOCK

WHITNEY, AMOS
New York, N. Y.
c. 1800-1810

A WHITNEY

WHITNEY, EBEN (W)
New York, N. Y.
w. 1805-1828

E.WHITNEY.

Whitney

WHITNEY, M. F.
Schenectady, N. Y.
w. 1823

M.WHITNEY

WHITNEY & HOYT (W)
New York, N. Y.
w. 1827-1836

WHITNEY&HOYT

WHITON, EZRA
Boston, Mass.
1813-1879

E.Whiton.

E.Whiton

WHITTAKER & GREEN
Providence, R. I.
1825

WHITTEMORE, WILLIAM
Portsmouth, N. H.
1710-1770

Whittemore

Whittmore

WICKHAM, DANIEL H.
New York, N. Y.
1835

WIGHTMAN, WILLIAM
Charleston, S. C.
w. 1783-*c.* 1825

WILCOX, A. D.
Troy, N. Y.
c. 1845

A.D.WILCOX

WILCOX, MICHAEL
Maryland
1772-1799

XXXX

WILLARD, A.
Utica, N. Y.
1810

AWILLARD   Utica

WILLARD & HAWLEY
Syracuse, N. Y.
c. 1850

WILLARD & HAWLEY

PREMIUM   SYRACUSE

WILLARD, JAMES
E. Windsor, Conn.
1815

WILLARD

WILLCOX, ALVAN
New Haven, Conn.
1783-1865

WILLCOX, CYPRIAN
New Haven, Conn.
1795-1875

C.WILCOX

WILLEY, B.
c. 1790

B.WILLEY

WILLIAMS, ALEXANDER
Philadelphia, Pa.
1807

WILLIAMS, CHARLES M.
New York, N. Y.
1825

WILLIAMS, DEODAT
Hartford, Conn.
w. 1776, *d.* 1781

WILLIAMS, JOHN
Philadelphia, Pa.
1793

J.Williams

WILLIAMS, STEPHEN
Providence, R. I.
1799

S.WILLIAMS

WILLIAMS, WM. A.
Washington, D. C.
1787-1846

W.A.WILLIAMS

WILLIAMSON, SAMUEL
Philadelphia, Pa.
1794

S·W SW WILLIAMSON

WILLIS, ANDREW
Boston, Mass.
1842

Andrew Willis
oppo. Old South

WILLIS, J.
Boston, Mass.
1820

WILLIS, STILLMAN
Boston, Mass.
w. 1813-1825

S.WILLIS

WILLIS, WILLIAM S.
Boston, Mass.
c. 1825

Wᵐ SWillis   Oppo4 Sou6

WILLS, HENRY
New York, N. Y.
1774

WILMOT, SAMUEL
New Haven, Conn.
1777-1846

S.WILMOT WILMOT

WILMOT, SAMUEL, JR.
New Haven, Conn.
1808-1846

WILMOT

WILMOT & STILLMAN
New Haven, Conn.
1800

WILMOT, THOMAS T.
Charleston, S. C.
w.c. 1837-1841

T.T.WILMOT
S.+T.T WILMOT

WILSON, ALBERT
Troy, N. Y.
1834

WILSON, EDWIN F.
Rochester, N. Y.
1838

WILSON, GEORGE
Philadelphia, Pa.
1850

WILSON, HOSEA
Philadelphia, Pa.
1812

H.WILSON   H WILSON

WILSON, HOSEA, & CO.
Baltimore, Md.
1814-1816

H WILSON & C°.

WILSON, JAMES
Trenton, N. J.
1769

WILSON, JOHN
Philadelphia, Pa.
1770

WILSON, R & W
Philadelphia, Pa.
w. 1825-1846

R&W.W   R&W.W
R&W.WILSON

WILSON, ROBERT
New York, N. Y.
Philadelphia, Pa.
w. 1808-1846

R.WILSON

R·W

WILSON, S.
Philadelphia, Pa.
1805

WILSON, S. & S.
Philadelphia, Pa.
1805

S.&S.WILSON

WILSON, THOMAS
Philadelphia, Pa.
1837

WILSON & TOY
Abingdon, Md.
1790

W.W   I.T

WILSON, WILLIAM
Philadelphia, Pa.
1755-1829

W.W

WILTBERGER & ALEXANDER
Philadelphia, Pa.
1797

WILTBERGER, CHRISTIAN
Philadelphia, Pa.
1766 1851

C.Wiltberger
C.Wiltberger

WINCHELL, V.

V.Winchell   PURE,COIN.

WINDOVER, JOHN
New York, N. Y.
1694

WING, MOSES
Windsor, Conn.
Worcester, Mass.
1760-1809

M.WING

WINSLOW, EDWARD
Boston, Mass.
1669-1753

WINSOR, WILLIAM
Boston, Mass.
1759

WISHART, ALEXANDER
New York, N. Y.
1808

WISHART, DANIEL
New York, N. Y.
1825

WISHART, HUGH
New York, N. Y.
w. 1784-1810

H.WISHART
WISHART

WISHART, WILLIAM
New York, N. Y.
1800

WITHINGTON, DANIEL
Ashland, O.
w. 1840

WITTICH, C. & F.
Charleston, S. C.
1802-1807

C.F.WITTICH

WITTICH, CHARLES
Charleston, S. C.
w. 1785-c. 1804

WOLCOTT & GELSTON
Boston, Mass.
1820-1830

Wolcott & Gelston

WOLCOTT, S. B.
S.B.WOLCOTT
PURE COIN

WOLF, I. (J)
Philadelphia, Pa.
w. 1828-1833

I.WOLF

WOLF, JAMES
Philadelphia, Pa.
b.c. 1775, w. 1831

I.WOLFF

WOLFE, FRANCIS H.
Philadelphia, Pa.
1829

FHWOLFE

WOLFE & WRIGGINS
Philadelphia, Pa.
1837

WOLFE & WRIGGINS

WOOD, A. & W.
New York, N. Y.
1850

A&W WOOD

WOOD, ALFRED
1800

WOOD

WOOD, BENJ. B.
New York, N. Y.
w. 1815-1846

WOOD & HUGHES
New York, N. Y.
w. 1840-1845

WOOD, J. E.
New York, N. Y.
1845

WOOD, JACOB
New York, N. Y.
w. 1834-1841

WOOD, JOHN
New York, N. Y.
w. 1770-1792

WOODCOCK, BANCROFT
Wilmington, Del.
w.c. 1754-1772

WOODCOCK & BURNS
Wilmington, Del.
1793

WOODCOCK, ISAAC
Wilmington, Del.
c. 1787

WOODRUFF, ENOS
Cincinnati, Ohio
1829

WOODRUFF & WHITE
Cincinnati, Ohio
1829

WOODS, FREEMAN
New York, N. Y.
w. 1791

WOODS, I.
c. 1790

WOODWARD, ANTIPAS
Middletown, Conn.
b. 1763, *w.* 1792

WOODWARD, CHARLES
New York, N. Y.
1825

WOODWARD, ELI
Boston, Mass.
1812

WOODWARD & GROSJEAN
Boston, Mass.
w. 1847-1852

WOODWORTH, E.
c. 1800

WOOL, JEREMIAH W.
New York, N. Y.
w. 1791

WRIGGIN & CO.
Philadelphia, Pa.
1831

WRIGGINS, THOMAS
Philadelphia, Pa.
1837

WRIGHT, ALEXANDER
Maryland
1776

WRIGHT, JOHN F.
Philadelphia, Pa.
1831

WRIGHT, WILLIAM
Charleston, S. C.
after 1743

(W. Wright)

WYATT, JOSEPH
Philadelphia, Pa.
1797

JW

WYER, ELEAZER, SR.
Portland, Me.
1750-1800

WYER, ELEAZER, JR.
Portland, Me.
1786-1848

E.WYER E.WYER

WYER & FARLEY
Portland, Me.
1828-1832

WYER & NOBLE
Portland, Me.
1823

WYNKOOP, BENJAMIN
New York, N. Y.
1675-1728

WK W.K.
B

WYNKOOP, BENJAMIN, JR.
New York, N. Y.
1705-1766

BW

WYNKOOP, CORNELIUS
New York, N. Y.
w. 1724-1740

WYNKOOP, JACOBUS
Kingston, N. Y.
1765

WYNKOOP

WYNN, CHRISTOPHER
Baltimore, Md.
1795-1883

C.WYNN.

Y

YATES, S.
Albany, N. Y.
c. 1810-1825

[S:YATES]

YEOMANS, ELIJAH
Hadley, Mass.
1738-1794

YETTONS, RANDELL
Philadelphia, Pa.
1739

YOU, DANIEL
Charleston, S. C.
w. 1744-1752

[DY] [DY]

YOU, THOMAS
Charleston, S. C.
w. 1753-1786

[TY]

YOUNG, ALEXANDER
Camden, S. C.
w. 1807-1856

[A·YOUNG]

YOUNG, EBENEZER
Hebron, Conn.
b. 1756, *w.* 1778

[YOUNG]

YOUNG, LEVI
Bridgeport, Conn.
1827

YOUNG, S. E.
Laconia, N. H.
1840

[SEYOUNG] [LACONIA NH]

YOUNG, WILLIAM
Philadelphia, Pa.
w. 1761-1784

[W. Young]

Z

ZAHN, G. M.
Lancaster, Pa.
1840

[GM·ZAHN]

ZAHM & JACKSON
New York, N. Y.
1830

[ZAHM & JACKSON]

ZANE, ISAAC
Zanesfield, O.
1795

[I.ZANE]

ZANE, JESSE
Wilmington, Del.
w. 1796

[J.ZANE]

SECTION TWO
AMERICAN PEWTER MARKS

American Pewter

PEWTER COLLECTING IN AMERICA has in recent years developed at an accelerated pace which can be attributed to at least three reasons. First, the dispersal of some of our leading collection (that of John B. Kerfoot, for instance) has heightened the interest of many novice collectors; research has clarified old issues and produced many new facts that are conducive to more leisurely and precise collecting. And thirdly, periodicals and books containing fresh evidence have appeared to throw new light on some points which have confused collectors. The enthusiast in this field is offered splendid opportunities to acquire a varied and representative assortment through continued search. A quest which would normally prove most tedious in other fields of American art is greatly enlivened by the ubiquitous nature of American pewter.

The actual composition of pewter is an interesting study in itself. There was no fixed proportion of the elements in old pewter. Its consistency varies from very soft and malleable to a hard, bright substance known as Britannia. In all cases, the basic ingredient is tin, to which was added copper, lead, bismuth, antimony, and in recent times, zinc. Depending upon the ultimate quality desired, those metals were added in varying quantities. For instance, in early continental pewter, copper alone was added to the tin base in perhaps a one to five proportion. Occasionally, this was combined with antimony, and with the addition of bismuth produced an alloy that was primarily used for plates, bowls, and other flatware. Later, lead found its way into pewter as a way of cheapening the metal itself and because it provided greater malleability. Early English pewter contained copper, then antimony in about a one to five proportion, progressing (or retrogressing) to a very low grade and low cost metal that had as much as a forty per cent lead content. In late eighteenth century America a representative specimen might contain the following components: eighty-nine per cent tin, eight per cent lead, two per cent antimony and about one per cent copper.

Towards the middle of the eighteenth century the English pewterers were finding porcelain and pottery gradually replacing their products in household use. To stimulate interest and increase the circulation of pewter some of the makers gave the trade name "Britannia" to their wares. That this movement eventually found its way into this country is evidenced by a considerable number of our early nineteenth century products.

Basically, Britannia metal differs vaguely from its pewter counterpart in only one respect, namely, a greater tin content. When this new name was applied its composition was the same as pewter, but gradually tin was used in increasing quantities, perhaps in an effort to compete with Sheffield-plate. The ultimate result was a tough, harsh-looking metal that lacked all of the full-rich qualities of older pewter. Thus, the use of Britannia was a transitional movement that has done nothing more than cause frequent conjecture over a trade name that was applied loosely to pewter in this later period.

Of course, large quantities of our early pewter have been regrettably destroyed, and much of it by the pewterers themselves. England was the prime source of tin and the American pewterer could ill afford to import this necessary ingredient. So he naturally took the easy way out and solicited old pieces that were worn or battered. These were always in abundance, for constant usage and longevity were not synonymous with that metal. Upon securing a sizable stock of antiquated utensils, he would recast them in their new form.

First, the proper mold would be selected and heated and then, after repeated castings, a very rough-looking product would result. At this point it was cut and filed to dispose of the excess metal, and then placed on a lathe. With the application of a cutting tool it began to assume its final appearance. The last step was burnishing or infrequently engraving or applying some other form of cut decoration. Hammering was also employed by many pewterers as a method of molding forms and also to increase the tensile strength. Teapots and similar hollow objects were made in two or more molds, and were then joined by soldering.

Pewter-making in China was an accomplished art more than one thousand years ago, and specimens have been unearthed in Europe that would indicate the presence of pewter fifteen hundred years ago. In 1473, Edward IV of England granted a charter to a pewterers' guild for the regulation and control of this craft. The early touch-plates on which each maker registered his touch or mark are still in existence. Life in those early times did not provide for any luxuries, so with the exception of the nobility, a pewter plate or mug was a cherished possession and one likely to be willed to the following generation. A communal spirit prevailed and food was eaten by hand from wooden plates or one or two large trenchers. Gradually, as the economy improved, pewter took the place of wood and by the end of the seventeenth century was quite commonplace even among the peasant classes. In America we find much the same situation, since wood was the predominant style until the early eighteenth century. The colonists became more aware of the changing customs of their neighbors across the sea; and slowly, in this more advanced society, the pewterer arose to take his place in the colonial pattern.

Of seventeenth century American pewterers very little is known for there are no records that would indicate there were more than a handful of men working here in that period. Among the earliest was one Richard Graves (1612-1669), of Salem, Massachusetts, who arrived here from England in 1635. Marked specimens of this period are practically non-existent. In the first half of the eighteenth century the same condition existed although the number of pewterers had increased considerably. The Revolutionary war was largely responsible for the dearth of marked examples of this era, for huge quantities were melted down to be recast into tools of war. The latter half of the eighteenth century, for all practical purposes marks the beginning of the period in which pieces by known craftsmen become available. It was during Revolutionary times that workers like Thomas Danforth II (1731-1782), David Melville (1755-1793), and Samuel Hamlin (1746-1801), were employed at their trade. Pewterers, following the example set by the early silversmiths, usually found themselves in the calling of their forebears. Thus, when Thomas Danforth opened his shop in Taunton, Massachusetts in 1727, the foundation was laid and the trade established for a long line of descendants. A brief genealogy of the members of this family who followed the trade is presented below.

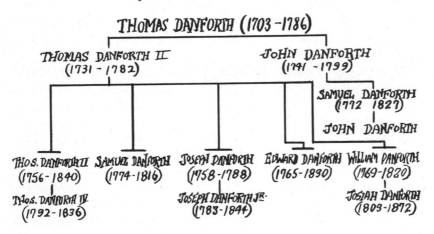

Another example of a family enterprise is that of the Boardmans, Thomas D. and Sherman, who served their apprenticeship under their uncle Samuel Danforth.

Determining the origin or age of American pewter is difficult if one were to judge by the form alone. Although pewter adapted itself to style changes there was no actual dividing line between one style and another. Most of the pewter that is still extant was made in the early nineteenth century, when the effects of social intercourse and more rapid transportation were first being felt. Even the smallest communities were no longer isolated from the outside world. This mundane movement tended to dissipate personal initiative in construction and to break down regional design. The result is a homogeneity that precludes the possibility of accurate attribution on shape alone. There were schools, however, that managed to retain their individual characteristics. Notable among these were the workers of Beverly, Mass. Specifically, the Trasks, Israel and Oliver, and their protegee, Eben Smith. Even here the dividing line draws thin for only a chiseled decoration in conjunction with form stability distinguishes their work from the group as a whole.

Even in the eighteenth century, before the refinements of civilization extended into the outermost hamlet, such an outstanding maker as William Will (1742-1798) was basing his designs on a composite of traditional forms. He and other craftsmen drew freely from the English and Continental standards and evolved, generally with some touch of individuality, a style that had found its origin many years before. As the mode of living changed the pewterer kept constant pace and form innovations were faithfully considered if not adopted. It must be admitted that, when examined as a whole, the ever-changing pattern presents a somewhat confusing picture to both historian and layman alike.

An important figure in Colonial America was the itinerant tradesman, who with horse and wagon and tinkling bells travelled throughout the rural areas bringing his wares and tidings of the outside world. For the urban pewterers this presented a way of disposing of their accumulated stock. For the itinerant tradesman it was a regular source of profit, for rare was the house that didn't have to replace battered pewter dishes or require some additional culinary article. And for a small sum the tradesman would arrange to melt down this old pewter and have it re-cast in a new and more desirable form. What with remolding by the many established makers, several American wars, and travelling pewterers, a lamentable paucity of early specimens results. This becomes apparent if the collector will consider the number of pieces he must first examine before coming upon even an "eagle touch," such as those in use at the turn of the century.

The matter of marking resolves itself into a comparatively simple problem. The early makers used marks or touches that are quite recognizable on the basis of the design alone. Unfortunately, through haste in application and wear, many are illegible, and many more were carelessly omitted entirely. The manner of marking periodically underwent great changes.

American pewter marks can be placed, generically, in three groups. The first can be roughly classed as pre-Revolutionary and were strongly influenced by English custom. Consisting commonly of the "Crown and Rose" and the "Lion Rampant" they were frequently used in conjunction with four (or less) square or shield-shaped "hall-marks" that carried no legal meaning whatsoever and did nothing more than simulate English marking. The wave of patriotism which overcame the colonies during and after the war was clearly reflected in the pewterers touches. For now the American eagle was commonly employed and such symbols as State coats-of-arms were used by New England pewterers. Finally, after 1825, with the approach of a mechanical era, individual names and places enclosed within rectangles, or incised, became the mode.

Identifying American pewter, with the exception of unmarked pieces, is seldom a difficult task, for the student and collector have a variety of tools at their disposal. First and foremost are the markings which can be easily checked against lists which are at this date fairly complete. Fraudulent touches are rarely encountered. However, these are quickly discernible. One situation that will always pose a problem was the marking of pieces with touches that were used by another member of the family, as in the case of the Samuel Hamlins.

Another means of identifying the approximate period of an object is through its particular function. For instance, porringers dating before 1800, although made in large quantities, are comparatively rare, and those dating after 1830 are equally scarce; beakers, except for their continued use in some churches, became obsolete at about 1815. While it is true that each successive period produced new designs, it would not be advisable to use these as the *sole* basis for identification, for many forms extended far into the following period.

As new states joined the union the pewterers gave them recognition through the addition of new stars to their touches, thus providing an interesting approach to establishing more specific dates. Through the calculation of the number of stars used in connection with the eagle touches of such men as the Danforths, George Lightner, and others, it is a simple process to determine roughly when the die for the touch itself was made.

The collector of American pewter is afforded ample opportunity to form a varied yet well-integrated collection through various sources. Most antique shops that specialize in Americana have on hand numerous specimens that are not only desirable as collector's pieces but as representative objects of an important age in our art-history. Splendid examples of eighteenth century pewter are frequently placed on sale by the larger auction galleries, and occasionally a rural auction will bring to light a rare and hitherto undiscovered piece. Considerable pewter is still in the hands of descendants of the original owners, and remains to be discovered for historical and other purposes.

A great stimulus to collecting is provided in all of these cases, for the discovery of a new touch, the unearthing of a rare piece by a known maker, or even the purchase of an ordinary teapot to fill an opening in a corner cupboard, will give the collector a feeling of satisfaction and accomplishment.

A

ALBERTI, JOHN PHILIP
Philadelphia, Pa.
w. 1754-1780

ALBERTI & HORAN
Philadelphia, Pa.
w.c. 1760

ALLAIRE, ANTHONY J.
New York, N. Y.
w.c. 1816-1821

ALLISON, ANDREW
New York, N. Y.
w. 1837-1841

ALLISON, JOHN
New York, N. Y.
w. 1835

ARCHER, BENJAMIN
St. Louis, Mo.
w. 1847

ARCHER, ELLIS S.
Philadelphia, Pa.
w.c. 1845

ARCHER & JANNEY
St. Louis, Mo.
1847

ARMITAGES & STANDISH
c. 1840

AUSTIN, JOHN
Boston, Mass.
w. 1785

AUSTIN, NATHANIEL
Charlestown, Mass.
1741-1816

AUSTIN, RICHARD
Boston, Mass.
w. 1792-1817

R·A·BOSTON

B

BABBITT, CROSSMAN & CO.
Taunton, Mass.
1826-1828

BABBITT & CROSSMAN
Taunton, Mass.
1814-1826

BADCOKE, THOMAS
Philadelphia, Pa.
d. 1707

BADGER, THOMAS, JR.
Boston, Mass.
1764-1826

BAILEY, TIMOTHY
Malden, Mass.
w. 1830-1840

BAILEY & PUTNAM
Malden, Mass.
c. 1830-1835

BAKER, JOHN
Boston, Mass.
1654-1696

BALDWIN, L. G.
Meriden, Conn.
w. 1849

BALL, WILLIAM
Philadelphia, Pa.
w. 1775-1782

BARNS, BLAKSLEE
Berlin, Conn.
w.c. 1805-1810
Philadelphia, Pa.
w. 1812-1817

BARNS, STEPHEN
Connecticut
c. 1795

BARTHOLDT, WILLIAM
Williamsburgh, N. Y.
w. 1850-1854

BARTON, CHARLES E.

Taunton, Mass.
c. 1835-1850

BASSETT, FRANCIS

New York, N. Y.
w. 1714-1758

BASSETT, FRANCIS, II

New York, N. Y.
w. 1754, d. 1800

The above touches may also have been used by Francis, Sr.

The above touch may also have been used by Frederick Bassett

BASSETT, FREDERICK

New York, N. Y.
1761-1780 and 1785-1800
Hartford, Conn.
1781-1785

BASSETT, JOHN

New York, N. Y.
w. 1720-1761

BELCHER, JOSEPH

Newport, R. I.
w.c. 1769-1776

BELCHER, JOSEPH, JR.

Newport, R. I.
w.c. 1776-1784
New London, Conn.
after 1784

The following touches may also have been used by Joseph, Sr.

BENEDICT, LEWIS
Albany, N. Y.
w. 1815-1824

BENHAM, MORRIS
West Meriden, Conn.
w. 1849

BENHAM & WHITNEY
New York, N. Y.
w. 1849

BILLINGS, WILLIAM
Providence, R. I.
w. 1791-1806

BILLINGS & DANFORTH
Providence, R. I.
1798-1801

BIRD, JAMES
New York, N. Y.
c. 1820

BLAND, JAMES
Westchester Co., N. Y.
c. 1760

BLIN, PETER
Boston, Mass.
b. 1733, *w.* 1759

BOARDMAN, HENRY S.
Hartford, Conn.
1841
Philadelphia, Pa.
c. 1844-1861

BOARDMAN
PHILAD⌐

BOARDMAN, J. D.
Hartford, Conn.
w. 1828

BOARDMAN, LUTHER
South Reading, Mass.
1836
Chester, Conn.
w. 1837-*c.* 1842

BOARDMAN, SHERMAN
Hartford, Conn.
w. 1810-1850

BOARDMAN, THOMAS D.
Hartford, Conn.
w. 1804-1850

X

BOARDMAN, T. D. & S.
Hartford, Conn.
w.c. 1810-1850

Pewter teapot with wooden handle, by William Will. (*Courtesy of The Metropolitan Museum of Art*).

BOARDMAN, TIMOTHY & CO.
(sales outlet for
T. D. & S. Boardman)
New York, N. Y.
1822-1825

BOARDMAN & CO. (same as above)
New York, N. Y.
1825-1827

BOARDMAN & HALL (same as above)
Philadelphia, Pa.
c. 1845

BOARDMAN & HART (same as above)
New York, N. Y.
1827-1850

BONNING, ROBERT
Boston, Mass.
w. 1739

BOUIS, JOHN
Baltimore, Md.
w. 1829-1834

BOUIS, JOHN AND SON
Baltimore, Md.
w. 1831

BOUIS, JOSEPH
Baltimore, Md.
w. 1834

BONZIGUES
Philadelphia, Pa.
c. 1810

BOWLES, SAMUEL
Boston, Mass.
w. 1787

BOWMAN, NATHANIEL
Charlestown, Mass.
w. 1806-1814

BOYD, PARKS
Philadelphia, Pa.
1797-1819

BOYLE, ROBERT
New York, N. Y.
w. 1753-1758

BRADFORD, CORNELIUS
New York, N. Y.
w. 1752, 1770-1785
Philadelphia, Pa.
w. 1758-1770

BRADFORD, JOHN
Boston, Mass.
w. 1784-1788

BRADFORD, WILLIAM
New York, N. Y.
w. 1719, *d.* 1758

BRADFORD & McEUEN
New York, N. Y.
1772-1786

BRIGDEN, TIMOTHY
Albany, N. Y.
w.c. 1816-1819

BROOK FARM
West Roxbury, Mass.
c. 1845

BROOKS, DAVID S.
Hartford, Conn.
w. 1828

BROWE & DOUGHERTY
Newark, N. J.
1845

BRUNSTROM, JOHN A.
Philadelphia, Pa.
w. 1783-1793

BUCKLEY, TOWNSEND M.
Troy, N. Y.
c. 1855

BULL, LYMAN & COUCH
Meriden, Conn.
1845-1849

BUMSTEED, THOMAS
Roxbury, Mass.
Boston, Mass.
w.c. 1640-1677

BURDETT, AARON
Baltimore, Md.
c. 1840

BYLES, THOMAS
Philadelphia, Pa.
w. 1738-1771

C

CAHILL, J. W. & CO.
c. 1835

CALDER, WILLIAM
Providence, R. I.
w.c. 1817-1856

CALVERLEY, JOHN
Philadelphia, Pa.
c. 1840

CAMP, WILLIAM E.
Middletown, Conn.
w. 1849

CAMPBELL, JOHN
Annapolis, Md.
1749-1770

CAMPBELL, MUNGO
Philadelphia, Pa.
c. 1752

CAMPMELL, (CAMPBELL) SAM'L
c. 1820

CAPEN, EPHRAIM
New York, N. Y.
c. 1848

E·CAPEN

CAPEN & MOLINEUX
New York, N. Y.
1848-1854

CARNES, JOHN
Boston, Mass.
1698-1760

Top: teapot with wooden handle, by William Will. (*Courtesy of Philadelphia Museum of Art*). Bottom: another teapot by William Will. (*Courtesy of The Metropolitan Museum of Art*).

CARTER, SAMUEL
Boston, Mass.
w.c. 1712-1747

CLARK(E), JONES
Boston, Mass.
b. 1690, *d.c.* 1760

CLARK(E), THOMAS
Boston, Mass.
1674-1720

COLDWELL, GEORGE
New York, N. Y.
w.c. 1789-1810

COLTON, OREN
Philadelphia, Pa.
c. 1835

O.COLTON

COMER, JOHN
Boston, Mass.
w.c. 1674-1721

COMER, JOHN JR.
Boston, Mass.
1674-1706

CONE, S. L.
Meriden, Conn.
c. 1849

CONNELL, THOMAS
Philadelphia, Pa.
w. 1829-1840

COPELAND, JOSEPH
Chuckatuck & Jamestown, Va.
w.c. 1675-1691

CORNE, ANTHONY
Charleston, S. C.
w. 1735

COX, WILLIAM
Philadelphia, Pa.
w. 1715-1721

CROSSMAN, WEST & LEONARD
Taunton, Mass.
1828-1830

CROSSMAN
WEST & LEONARD

CURTIS, EDWIN E.
Meriden, Conn.
w. 1838-1845

CURTIS, ENOS H.
Meriden, Conn.
c. 1845

CURTIS, LEMUEL J.
Meriden, Conn.
w. 1836-1849

L.J.CURTISS

CURTIS & CURTIS (E. E. & L. J.)
Meriden, Conn.
1838-1840

Domed top tankard by Francis Bassett II. (*Courtesy, Brooklyn Museum*).

Spoon by William Kirby. (*Courtesy, Brooklyn Museum*).

Writing box by Henry Will. (*Courtesy, Brooklyn Museum*).

CURTIS & LYMAN
Meriden, Conn.
from 1846

CURTISS, DANIEL
Albany, N. Y.
w. 1822-1850

CURTISS, I.
c. 1820

CURTISS, JOSEPH
Troy, N. Y.
w. 1827-1832
Albany, N. Y.
w. 1832-1859

CUTLER, DAVID
Boston, Mass.
1703-1772

D

DANFORTH, EDWARD
Middletown, Conn.
w.c. 1788
Hartford, Conn.
c. 1790

DANFORTH, JOB
Providence, R. I.
w. 1798-1801

DANFORTH, JOHN
Norwich, Conn.
w. 1773-1793

DANFORTH, JOSEPH
Middletown, Conn.
w. 1782-1788

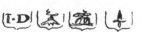

DANFORTH, JOSEPH, JR.

Richmond, Va.
w.c. 1807-*c.* 1812

DANFORTH, JOSIAH

Middletown, Conn.
w.c. 1825-1837

DANFORTH, SAMUEL

Norwich, Conn.
w. 1793-1803

DANFORTH, SAMUEL

Hartford, Conn.
w. 1795-1816

DANFORTH, THOMAS

Taunton, Mass.
w. 1727-1733
Norwich, Conn.
w. 1733-1773

Left to right: pewter teapot by William Kirby; baptismal bowl by Samuel Danforth, dish by Thomas Danforth I and his son, John; sugar bowl attributed to Johann C. Heyne. (*All photos Courtesy of The Metropolitan Museum of Art*).

Left to right: chalice by Johann C. Heyne; fifteen-inch hammered dish by Simon Edgell; two-quart flagon by Thomas Danforth Boardman and Sherman Boardman. (*Courtesy of The Metropolitan Museum of Art*).

DANFORTH, THOMAS II

Middletown, Conn.
w. 1755-1782

DANFORTH, THOMAS III

Rocky Hill, Conn.
w. 1777-c. 1818
Philadelphia, Pa.
w. 1807-1813

DANFORTH, THOMAS IV

Philadelphia, Pa.
b. 1792, d. 1836

DANFORTH, WILLIAM

Middletown, Conn.
w. 1792-1820

DAY, BENJAMIN

Newport, R. I.
b.c. 1706, d. 1757

DERBY, THOMAS S.

Middletown, Conn.
w.c. 1818-c. 1850

DERBY, THOMAS S., JR.

Middletown, Conn.
w.c. 1840-1850

DERBY, THOMAS S. & SON

Middletown, Conn.
c. 1849

DE RIEMER, CORNELIUS B. & Co

Auburn, N. Y.
c. 1835

C.B. DE RIEMER &Cº
AUBURN

DIGGS, WILLIAM
New York, N. Y.
c. 1702

DOLBEARE, EDMUND
Boston, Mass.
w. 1671-*c.* 1705

DOLBEARE, JAMES
Boston, Mass.
b. 1705-*d.* before 1775

DOLBEARE, JOHN
Boston, Mass.
b.c. 1664-*w.* to 1740

DOLBEARE, JOSEPH
Boston, Mass.
w.c. 1690-*c.* 1704

DUNHAM, E.
after 1825

DUNHAM, RUFUS
Westbrook, Me.
w. 1837-1861

R. DUNHAM

DUNHAM, R. & SONS
Portland, Me.
1861-1882

DURNINGER, DANIEL
Boston, Mass.
w. 1723

E

EDGELL, SIMON
Philadelphia, Pa.
w. 1713-1742

EDGELL, WILLIAM
Boston, Mass.
w. 1724

EGGLESTON, JACOB
Middletown, Conn.
w. 1796-1807
Fayetteville, N. C.
w. 1807-1813

ELDREDGE, ELI
Boston, Mass., 1849
Taunton, Mass., 1860

ELLISON, JOHN (ALLISON?)
Philadelphia, Pa.
w. 1837

ELSWORTH, WILLIAM J.
New York, N. Y.
w. 1767-1798

The following touches are tentative-
ly attributed to Elsworth

ENDICOTT, EDMUND
New York, N. Y.
w. 1846-1853

E. ENDICOTT

ENDICOTT AND SUMNER
New York, N. Y.
1846-1851

ESTABROOK, RICHARD
Boston, Mass.
w.c. 1720

EVERETT, JAMES
Philadelphia, Pa.
w. 1716

F

FELTMAN, J. C., JR.
Albany, N. Y.
c. 1847

FENN, GAIUS & JASON
New York, N. Y.
w. 1831-1843

FIELDS, PHILIP
New York, N. Y.
c. 1799

FLAGG, ASA F.
Cincinnati, Ohio
w. 1842-1854

FLAGG, DAVID
Boston, Mass.
w. before 1750-1772

FLAGG AND HOMAN
Cincinnati, Ohio
1842-1854

FLETCHER, THOMAS
Philadelphia, Pa.
c. 1840

FRANCIS, DANIEL
Buffalo, N. Y.
w. 1835-1842

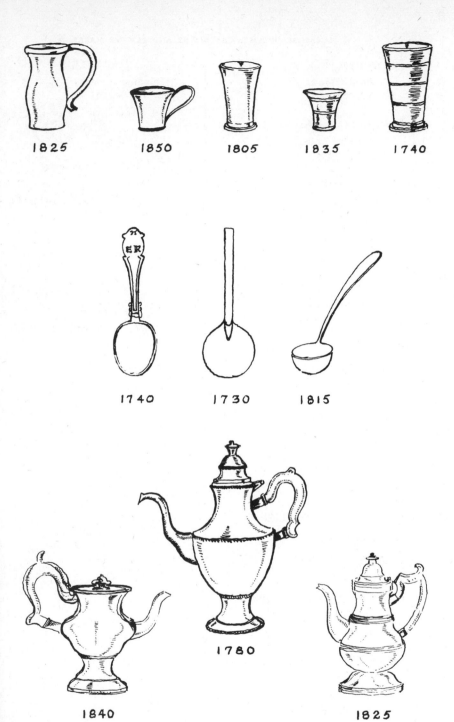

1825   1850   1805   1835   1740

1740   1730   1815

1780

1840   1825

FRANCIS, THOMAS
Boston, Mass.
w. 1718

FRARY, JAMES A.
Meriden, Conn.
w. 1845-1849

FRARY AND BENHAM
Meriden, Conn.
c. 1849

FRYERS, JOHN
Newport, R. I.
b.c. 1685, *d.* 1776

FULLER AND SMITH
New London, Conn.
c. 1850

G

————Y AND GARDNER
after 1830

GEANTY, LEWIS
Baltimore, Md.
c. 1800

GEORGE, ANTHONY, JR.
Philadelphia, Pa.
w. 1839-1847

GERHARDT & CO.
after 1840

GERHARDT
& CO.

GLEASON, ROSWELL
Dorchester, Mass.
w. 1822-1871

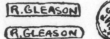

ROSWELL GLEASON

GLENNORE CO. (see under G.
RICHARDSON)

GRAME, SAMUEL
Boston, Mass.
w.c. 1639-1645

GRAVES, HENRY H.
Middletown, Conn.
c. 1850

H.H.GRAVES

GRAVES, JOSHUA B.
Middletown, Conn.
c. 1849

J.B.GRAVES

GRAVES, J. B. AND H. H.
Middletown, Conn.
w. 1852

J.B.&H.H.GRAVES

GRAVES, RICHARD
Salem, Mass.
w. 1635-1667

GREEN, ANDREW
Boston, Mass.
w. 1773-*c.* 1798

GREEN, JONAS
Boston, Mass.
w.c. 1787

Left: porringer by Samuel Hamlin. Right: dish by Thomas Danforth III. (*Both photos Courtesy of Philadelphia Museum of Art*).

GREEN, SAMUEL
Boston, Mass.
w.c. 1778-*c.* 1830

GREEN, SAMUEL, JR.
Boston, Mass.
w.c. 1821-*c.* 1835

GREEN, THOMAS
Boston, Mass.
1715-1794

GREEN, THOMAS, JR.
Boston, Mass.
b. 1746, *d.c.* 1790

GREEN, TIMOTHY
Boston, Mass.
w. 1780

GREEN AND AUSTIN
Boston, Mass.
1812-1817

GREEN AND RICHARDSON
Boston, Mass.
1818

GRINDELL (GRENNELL),
THOMAS)
New York, N. Y.
c. 1790

GRISWOLD, ASHBIL
Meriden, Conn.
w. 1807-1842

A.G

GRISWOLD, GILES
Augusta, Ga.
c. 1820

GRISWOLD, SYLVESTER
Baltimore, Md.
c. 1820

GRISWOLD AND COUCH
Meriden, Conn.
c. 1830

H

HALL, FRANKLIN D.
Hartford, Conn.
c. 1840
Philadelphia, Pa.
w. 1842-1857

HALL, JOHN H.
Middletown, Conn.
c. 1815

HALL, BOARDMAN & CO.
Philadelphia, Pa.
1846-1848

HALL AND BOARDMAN
Philadelphia, Pa.
1849-1857

HALL AND COTTON
c. 1840

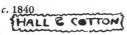

HALL, ELTON AND CO.
Wallingford, Conn.
c. 1860

HAMLIN, SAMUEL
Providence, R. I.
w.c. 1771-1801

HAMLIN, SAMUEL E.
Providence, R. I.
w. 1801-1856

HAMLIN AND JONES
Providence, R. I.
1774-1781

HARBESON, (BENJ., JOS., OR ROB'T)
Philadelphia, Pa.
c. 1800

HARNER, GEORGE
New York, N. Y.
c. 1761

HARRISON, JOSEPH
Philadelphia, Pa.
w. 1829-1852

HART, LUCIUS D.
New York, N. Y.
w. 1828-1850

HASSELBERG, ABRAHAM
Philadelphia, Pa.
w. 1762-1779

HENDRICKS, FRANCIS G.
Charleston, S. C.
w. 1771-*c.* 1784

HENRY, ANDREW
Orange Co., N. Y.
c. 1761

HERA, CHRISTIAN
Philadelphia, Pa.
w. 1791-1817

HERA, C. & J.
Philadelphia, Pa.
1800-1812

HERA, JOHN
Philadelphia, Pa.
w. 1800-1812

HERA, JOHN, JR.
Philadelphia, Pa.
w. 1817-1821

HERS ———, S. S.
after 1825

HEYNE, JOHANN C.
Lancaster, Pa.
w. 1754-1780

HILL, JOHN
New York, N. Y.
w. 1847

HILLSBURGH, CHARLES
New York, N. Y.
w. 1837

HINSDALE, JOHN & DANIEL
(Retailers)
Middletown, Conn.
c. 1815

HOLMES, ROBERT, & SONS
Baltimore, Md.
w. 1853

HOLMES & SONS
BALTIMORE

HOLT, THOMAS R.
Meriden, Conn.
w. 1845-1849

T.R.HOLT   T·R·H·

HOLYOKE, JOHN
Boston, Mass.
1683-1775

HOMAN, HENRY
Cincinnati, O.
w. 1847-1854

H. HOMAN

HOMAN & CO. (HOMAN & FLAGG)
Cincinnati, O.
1847-1854

HOMAN & CO.
CINCINNATI

HOPPER, HENRY
New York, N. Y.
w. 1842-1847

HORAN, JOHANN C.
Philadelphia, Pa.
w. 1754-1785

HORSEWELL, WILLIAM
New York, N. Y.
c. 1707

HORSFORD, E. N.
after 1830

E.N. HORSFORD'S
PATENT

HOUGHTON AND WALLACE
Philadelphia, Pa.
c. 1843

HOUGHTON
&
WALLACE

HOUSE, EDWIN
Hartford, Conn.
w. 1841-1846

HUMISTON, WILLIS
Troy, N. Y.
c. 1840

HUNT, S.
after 1830

S HUNT

HUNTER, GEORGE
Troy, N. Y.
w. 1831

HYDE, MARTIN
New York, N. Y.
w. 1857

M. HYDE

D. M. H.
after 1830

DMH

I

ISLY, JOSEPH
New York, N. Y.
c. 1710

J

JACKSON, JONATHAN
Boston, Mass.
1672-1736

JAGGER, DANIEL H.
Hartford, Conn.
c. 1845

JAGGER, JAMES H.
Hartford, Conn.
w. 1843

JAGGER, WALTER W.
Hartford, Conn.
w. 1839-1846

JENNINGS, THEODORE
Maryland
c. 1775

JOHNSON, JEHIEL
Middletown, Conn.
w. 1815-1825
Fayetteville, N. C.
w.c. 1818

JOHNSON, HALL & CO.
Middletown, Conn.
1815-1817

JOHNSON & MOTT
Middletown, Conn.
1817-1819

JONES, DANIEL
Boston, Mass.
w. 1714

JONES, EDWARD
New York, N. Y.
w. 1837-1850

JONES, GERSHOM
Providence, R. I.
w. 1774-1809

JONES, GERSHOM, & SONS
Providence, R. I.
c. 1806

K

KEENE, JOSIAH
Providence, R. I.
w. 1801-c. 1817

KEHLER, ADAM
Philadelphia, Pa.
w.c. 1780

KIERSTED, LUKE
New York, N. Y.
c. 1805

Chalice by Johann C. Heyne.
(*Courtesy, Brooklyn Museum*)

"Lighthouse"
teapot by
Eben Smith.
(*Courtesy,
Brooklyn
Museum*).

KILBOURN, SAMUEL

Baltimore, Md.

w. 1814-1839

KILBOURN & PORTER

Baltimore, Md.

1814-1816

KIMBERLY, DEWITT

Meriden, Conn.

w. 1845-1849

KIRBY, PETER

New York, N. Y.

w.c. 1736-*c.* 1776

KIRBY, WILLIAM

New York, N. Y.

w.c. 1760-1794

KIRK, ELISHA

York, Pa.

c. 1785

KNAPP, ELIJAH

New York, N. Y.

w. 1797

KNEELAND, EDWARD

Boston, Mass.

w.c. 1768-*c.* 1791

KNIGHT, W. W., & CO. (Retailer?)

Philadelphia, Pa.

c. 1840

W.W. KNIGHT & CO.

KRUIGER, LEWIS

Philadelphia, Pa.

w. 1833

L. KRUIGER PHILAD

L

LAFETRA, MOSES

New York, N. Y.

w. 1811-1816

LAFETRA & ALLAIRE

New York, N. Y.

c. 1816

LANGWORTHY, LAWRENCE
Newport, R. I.
w.c. 1730-1739

LATHBURY, JOHN
Virginia
1655

LEDDELL, JOSEPH
New York, N. Y.
w.c. 1711-1753

LEDDELL, JOSEPH, JR.
New York, N. Y.
w.c. 1740-1754

The above touches may also have been used by Joseph, Sr.

LEE, RICHARD
Grafton, N. H., *w.* 1788-1790
Ashfield, Mass., 1791-1793
Lanesborough, Mass., 1794-1802
Springfield, Vt., 1802-1823

LEE, RICHARD, JR.
Springfield, Vt.
w.c. 1795-*c.* 1815

The above touch was also used by Richard Lee, Sr.

LEONARD, REED & BARTON
Taunton, Mass.
1835-1840

LEONARD REED & BARTON

LESLIE, ELKINS
Philadelphia, Pa., *c.* 1821
Providence, R. I., *w.* 1828

LEWIS, ISAAC C.
Meriden, Conn.
w. 1834-1852

I.C.LEWIS

LEWIS, I. C. & CO.
Meriden, Conn.
1839-1852

ICL & CO.

LEWIS & COWLES
East Meriden, Conn.
1834-1836

LEWIS & MERIDEN COWLES

LEWIS & CURTIS
East Meriden, Conn.
1836-1839

LIGHTNER, GEORGE
Baltimore, Md.
w.c. 1806-1815

LOCKE, J. D.
New York, N. Y.
w. 1835-*c.* 1860

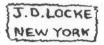

LOCKE & CARTER
New York, N. Y.
1837-1845

LOVE, I.
Baltimore, Md.
after 1840

I. LOVE

LOWE, I.
after 1800

LYMAN, WILLIAM W.
Meriden, Conn.
1844-1852

LYMAN

LYMAN & COUCH
Meriden, Conn.
w. 1844

M

MANN (MAN), WILLIAM
Boston, Mass.
w.c. 1690-*c.* 1738

MANNING, E. B.
Middletown, Conn.
w.c. 1850-*c.* 1865

E.B.MANNING
PATENT

MANNING, THADDEUS
Middletown, Conn.
w. 1849

MANNING, BOWMAN & CO.
Middletown, Conn.
w. 1866

MANNING BOWMAN & CO

MARSTON
Baltimore, Md.
after 1830

MARSTON.
BALTIMORE.

MATON, MARCUS
Hartford, Conn.
w. 1828

McEUEN, DUNCAN
New York, N. Y.
w. 1793-1798

McEUEN, MALCOLM
New York, N. Y.
w. 1770-1798

McEUEN, MALCOLM & DUNCAN
New York, N. Y.
1793-1798

1840   1835   1850   1775

1840   1830   1840   1845

1790 1790 1770 1765 1825 1825

1745   1815   1780   1790   1820

1810   1760   1780   1780   1780

1810

McILMOY, JOHN
Philadelphia, Pa.
w. 1793

McQUILKIN, WILLIAM
Philadelphia, Pa.
w. 1845-1853

MELVILLE, ANDREW
Newport, R. I.
w. 1805-1810

MELVILLE, DAVID
Newport, R. I.
1755-1793

DXM
1788

MELVILLE, SAMUEL
Newport, R. I.
w.c. 1793-1800

MELVILLE, S. & T.
Newport, R. I.
w.c. 1793-1800

MELVILLE, THOMAS
Newport, R. I.
w.c. 1793-1796

MELVILLE, THOMAS, JR.
Newport, R. I.
w. 1796-1824

The following touch was also used by Thomas, Sr.

T M

MELVILLE, WILLIAM L.
Newport, R. I.
1786-1857

MERIDEN BRITANNIA CO.
Meriden, Conn.
from 1852

MERIDEN
BRITANNIA
CO.

MERRYFIELD, ROBERT
New York, N. Y.
c. 1760

MICHEL, ANDRE
New York, N. Y.
w. 1795-1797

MIX, G. I. & CO.
Yalesville, Conn.
after 1860

MOORE, LUKE
Philadelphia, Pa.
c. 1820

MOREY & OBER
Boston, Mass.
1852-1855

MOREY, OBER AND CO.
Boston, Mass.
1855-1857

MOREY & SMITH
Boston, Mass.
1857-1885

MORGAN, HENRY
Groton, Conn.
w. 1849

MUNSON, JOHN
Yalesville, Conn.
w. 1846-1852

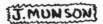

N

NEAL, I.
c. 1842

NORSWORTH, JOHN
Norfolk, Va.
w. 1771

NORTH & ROWE
Augusta, Ga.
1818-1823

NORTHEY, DAVID
Salem, Mass.
w. 1732-1778

NORTHEY, WILLIAM
Lynn, Mass.
b.c. 1734-*d.* 1804

NOTT, WILLIAM
Philadelphia, Pa.
c. 1812

Typical pewter of New York and Massachusetts, 18th Century. (*Courtesy of The Metropolitan Museum of Art*).

Typical pewter of Pennsylvania, Connecticut and New York, 18th Century. (*Courtesy of The Metropolitan Museum of Art*).

NOTT, WILLIAM
Middletown, Conn.
w. 1813-1817
Fayetteville, N. C.
1817-1825

NOTT, BABCOCK & JOHNSON
Middletown, Conn.
c. 1817

O

OLCOTT, J. W.
Baltimore, Md.
c. 1800

OSTRANDER, CHARLES
New York, N. Y.
w. 1848-1854

OSTRANDER & NORRIS
New York, N. Y.
1848-1850

P

PALETHORP, JOHN H.
Philadelphia, Pa.
w. 1820-1845

PALETHORP, ROBERT
Philadelphia, Pa.
w. 1822-1825

PALETHORP, ROBERT, JR.
Philadelphia, Pa.
w. 1817-1822

PALETHORP, R. & J. H.
Philadelphia, Pa.
1820-1826

PALETHORP & CONNELL
Philadelphia, Pa.
1839-1841

PALETHORP
B.CONNELL

PHILADª

PARKER, CHARLES & CO.
Meriden, Conn.
c. 1850

C.PARKER & CO.

PARKER, J. G.
Rochester, N. Y.
c. 1840

PARKIN, W.
after 1830

W. PARKIN

PARMENTER, W. H.
after 1840

PASCHALL, THOMAS
Philadelphia, Pa.
w. 1686-1718

PAVEY, GEORGE
Boston, Mass.
w. 1733

PEEL, HENRY
Philadelphia, Pa.
w. 1822-1833

PIERCE, SAMUEL
Greenfield, Mass.
w.c. 1792-c. 1831

PIERCE, ROBERT
New York, N. Y.
w. 1792-1797

PLUMLY (PLUMLEY), CHARLES
Providence, R. I., c. 1829
Middletown, Conn.
w. 1844-1848

PLUMLY & BIDGOOD
Philadelphia, Pa.
c. 1825

PORTER, ALLEN
Westbrook, Me.
w. 1830-1840

PORTER, A. & F. ·
Westbrook, Me.
1835-1840

PORTER BRITANNIA & PLATE CO.
Taunton, Mass.
c. 1860

R

PORTER, FREEMAN
Westbrook, Me.
w. 1835-*c.* 1860

RAISIN, GEORGE
Boston, Mass.
w.c. 1718-1728

RANDLE, JOSEPH
Boston, Mass.
w. 1739

PORTER, JAMES
Baltimore, Md.
w.c. 1795-*c.* 1803

REED, HENRY G.
Taunton, Mass.
w. 1835-*c.* 1860

REED & BARTON
Taunton, Mass.
1840 to present day

REED & BARTON

REICH, JOHN P.
Salem, N. C.
w.c. 1820-1830

PORTER, JEPHTHA
Baltimore, Md.
w. 1814-1816

POTTER, W.
c. 1835

W. POTTER

REICH, J. & P.
Salem, N. C.
c. 1829

RENTON & CO.
New York, N. Y.
after 1830

RENTON & CO.
NEW YORK

PUTNAM, JAMES H.
Malden, Mass.
w. 1830-1855

PUTNAM

1770   1830   1810   1845

1830   1795   1750   1830

1810   1825   1780   1780

1810   1780   1840   1815

RICHARDSON, B. & SON
Philadelphia, Pa.
c. 1839

B. RICHARDSON & SON
PHILADELPHIA

RICHARDSON, FRANCIS
Providence, R. I.
c. 1847

RICHARDSON, GEORGE
Boston, Mass.
Cranston, R. I.
w.c. 1818-1845

G. RICHARDSON
BOSTON

RICHARDSON, GEORGE B.
Providence, R. I.
w. 1847-1848

RODGERS, JOHN
Philadelphia, Pa.
w. 1840

ROGERS, SMITH & CO.
Hartford, Conn.
c. 1850

RUSSELL & BEACH
Chester, Conn.
w. 1838

RUST, J. N. & S.
New York, N. Y.
1842-1845

RUST, LEONARD M.
New York, N. Y.
w. 1849

RUST, SAMUEL
New York, N. Y.
w. 1837-1845

S. RUSTS PATENT
NEW YORK

S

SAGE, TIMOTHY
St. Louis, Mo.
w. 1848

T. SAGE
ST. LOUIS, MO.

SAGE, T. & CO.
St. Louis, Mo.
w. 1847

SAGE & BEEBE
after 1840

SAGE & BEEBE

SAVAGE & GRAHAM

Middletown, Conn.

c. 1837

SAVAGE, WILLIAM H.

Middletown, Conn.

w. 1837-1840

SEIP, JACOB

Philadelphia, Pa.

c. 1820

SELLEW & CO.

Cincinnati, O.

1830-*c.* 1860

SELTZER, ABRAHAM

Philadelphia, Pa.

c. 1793

"SEMPER EADEM"

Boston, Mass.

c. 1760-*c.* 1780

SHELDON & FELTMAN

Albany, N. Y.

w. 1847-1848

SHOFF, I.

Pennsylvania

c. 1785

SHRIMPTON, HENRY

Boston, Mass.

b.c. 1615-1666

SICKEL & SHAW

Philadelphia, Pa.

w. 1850

SICKEL, H. G.

Philadelphia, Pa.

w. 1849-1853

SIMPKINS, THOMAS

Boston, Mass.
1702-1766

SIMPSON, SAMUEL

Yalesville, Conn.
New York, N.Y.
w. 1837-1852

SIMPSON & BENHAM

New York, N.Y.
1845-1847

SIMPSON
&
BENHAM

SKINNER, JOHN

Boston, Mass.
w.c. 1760-1790

SMITH, EBEN

Beverly, Mass.
w. 1841-*c.* 1856

SMITH, GEORGE W.

Albany, N.Y.
w. 1849-1856

SMITH, JAMES E.

after 1775

SMITH, OBER & CO.

Boston, Mass.
1849-1852

SMITH, THOMAS

Boston, Mass.
w. 1841-1862

SMITH, THOMAS

Boston, Mass.
w.c. 1700-1742

SMITH, THOMAS, & CO.

Baltimore, Md.
1842-1847

SMITH, WILLIAM R.

Middletown, Conn.
w. 1848

SMITH & CO.

Albany, N.Y.
1853-1856

SMITH & CO.

Boston, Mass.
1847-1849

SMITH & FELTMAN

Albany, N.Y.
1849-1852

SMITH & FELTMAN
ALBANY

SMITH & MOREY

Boston, Mass.
1841-1842

SOUTHMAYD, EBENEZER

Castleton, Vt.
w. 1802-*c.* 1830

STAFFORD, BENEDICT & CO.

Albany, N. Y.
1824

STAFFORD, SPENCER

Albany, N. Y.
w. 1794-1827

STAFFORD, S. & CO.

Albany, N. Y.
1817-1824

STAFFORD, SPENCER & CO.

Albany, N. Y.
1815-1817

STAFFORD & MINZE

Albany, N. Y.
c. 1795

STAFFORDS, ROGERS & CO.

Albany, N. Y.
1814-1815

STALKAMP, J. H. & CO.

Cincinnati, O.
w.c. 1850-1856

STANDISH, ALEXANDER

after 1835

ALEXᴱ STANDISH

STARR, WILLIAM H.

New York, N. Y.
w. 1843-1846

STEDMAN, S.

after 1800

S. STEDMAN

STEINMAN, J. F.

Lancaster, Pa.
w. 1783-1785

STODDARD, FREDERICK

Philadelphia, Pa.
w. 1833

SYKES
c. 1850

SYKES

T

TAUNTON BRITANNIA MFG. CO.
Taunton, Mass.
1830-1835

TAUNTON BRT²
MANF² CO

T. B. M. CO.

THOMAS, JOHN
Philadelphia, Pa.
w. 1841

THORNTON, JOHN
after 1774

TOMLINSON
c. 1843

TOMLINSON'S
PATENT,
1843

TRASK, ISRAEL
Beverly, Mass.
w.c. 1825-*c.* 1856

I·TRASK

TRASK, OLIVER
Beverly, Mass.
w.c. 1825-*c.* 1839

O.TRASK

TREADWAY, AMOS
Middletown, Conn.
w.c. 1785

TYLER, JOHN
Boston, Mass.
1695-1757

V

VOSE & CO.
Albany, N. Y.
after 1840

VOSE & CO.
ALBANY

W

WADSWORTH, LESTER
Hartford, Conn.
w. 1838

WALLACE, R. & Co.
Wallingford, Conn.
from 1855

R.WALLACE & CO.

WARD, H. B. & Co.
Wallingford, Conn.
c. 1849

H.B.WARD.

WARREN
after 1830

WARREN'S
HARD METAL

WAYNE, C. P. & SON
Philadelphia, Pa.
c. 1835

C.P.WAYNE & SON

PHILADª

WEEKES, JAMES
New York, N. Y.
from *c.* 1820
Poughkeepsie, N. Y.
from *c.* 1835

J.WEEKES

J.WEEKES NY

J. WEEKES
BROOKLYN

WEEKES, J. & Co.
Poughkeepsie, N. Y.
1833-1835

WEEKES & CO

WHITCOMB, A. G.
Boston, Mass.
after 1820

WHITEHOUSE, E.
after 1800

WHITEHOUSE

WHITEHOUSE
WARRANTED

WHITFIELD, GEORGE B.
New York, N. Y.
w. 1828-1865

WHITFIELD, G. & J.
New York, N. Y.
1836-1865

G.& J. WHITFIELD

WHITLOCK, JOHN H.
Troy, N. Y.
w. 1836-1844

WHITLOCK
TROY N.Y.

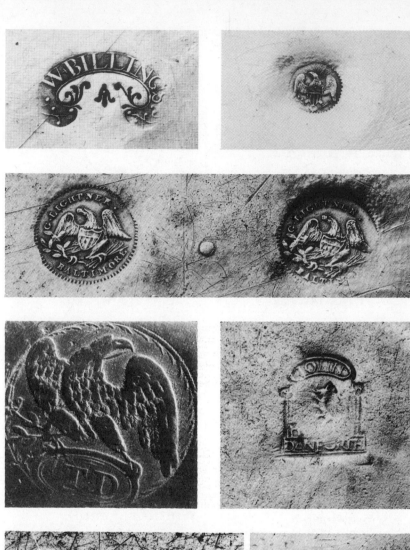

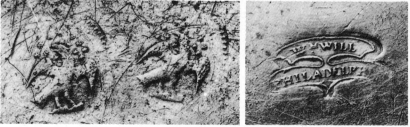

"Touches" on pewter by leading makers. (*Courtesy of The Metropolitan Museum of Art and Philadelphia Museum of Art*).

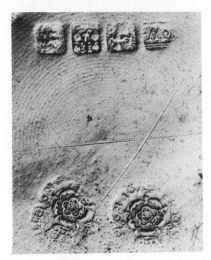

"Touches" on pewter by leading makers. (*Courtesy of The Metropolitan Museum of Art and Philadelphia Museum of Art*).

WHITMORE, JACOB
Middletown, Conn.
w.c. 1758-c. 1790

WHITMORE, LEWIS
Rocky Hill, Conn.
c. 1840

WHITMORE & FRANCIS
Buffalo, N. Y.
c. 1833

WILDS, THOMAS
Philadelphia, Pa.
w. 1829-1833

WILDES, THOMAS
New York, N. Y.
w. 1833-1840

WILL, CHRISTIAN
New York, N. Y.
w.c. 1770-1789

WILL, GEORGE W.
Philadelphia, Pa.
w. 1798-1807

WILL, HENRY
New York, N. Y.
w. 1761-1775; 1783-c. 1793
Albany, N. Y.
w. 1775-1783

WILL, JOHN
New York, N. Y.
w.c. 1752-c. 1763

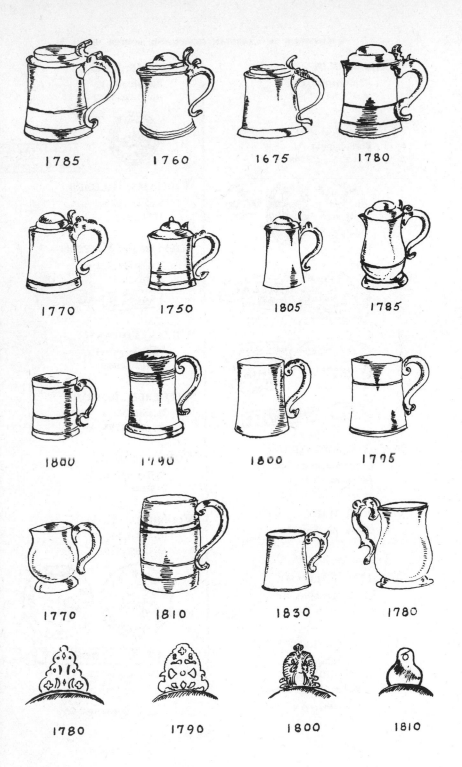

1785   1760   1675   1780

1770   1750   1805   1785

1800   1790   1800   1775

1770   1810   1830   1780

1780   1790   1800   1810

WILL, PHILIP
Philadelphia, Pa.
w. 1763-1787

WILL, WILLIAM
Philadelphia, Pa.
w.c. 1770, *d.* 1798

WILLETT, EDWARD
Upper Marlboro, Md.
w.c. 1692-1743

WILLETT, MARY
Upper Marlboro, Md.
c. 1773

WILLETT, WILLIAM
Upper Marlboro, Md.
w. 1744-1772

WILLIAMS, LORENZO L.
Philadelphia, Pa.
w. 1835-1842

L.L. WILLIAMS
PHILAD⁹

WILLIAMS, OTIS
Buffalo, N. Y.
w.c. 1826-1830

WILLIAMS, RICHARD
Stepney, Conn.
1771-1812

WILLIAMS & SIMPSON
Yalesville, Conn.
w. 1837

WILLIS, THOMAS
Philadelphia, Pa.
w. 1829-1833

WITHERLE, JOSHUA
Boston, Mass.
w. 1784-1793

WOLFE, JOHN B.
Philadelphia, Pa.
c. 1800

WOODBURY, J. B.
Philadelphia, Pa.
w. 1835-1836

1815   1765   1810

1825   1845   1820

1835   1840   1770

1775   1830   1820

1830   1830   1830

WOODBURY & COLTON
Philadelphia, Pa.
c. 1835

WOODBURY8 COLTON *

WOODMAN, COOK & CO.
Portland, Me.
after 1830

WOODMAN,COOK8CO.

WYER, SIMON
Philadelphia, Pa.
w. 1740-1752

Y

YALE, BURRAGE
So. Reading, Mass.
w.c. 1808-1835

YALE, CHARLES
Wallingford, Conn.
w.c. 1818-1835

YALE, C. & S.
Wallingford, Conn.
Richmond, Va.
w. 1817-1823

YALE, HIRAM
Wallingford, Conn.
w. 1822-1831

YALE, HIRAM & CO.
Yalesville, Conn.
1824-1835

YALE, SAMUEL
Meriden, Conn.
w.c. 1810-1820

YALE, SELDEN
Wallingford, Conn.
Richmond, Va.
w.c. 1817-1823

YALE, WILLIAM
Meriden, Conn.
w. 1813-1830
New York, N. Y.
w. 1830-1832

YALE, W. & S.
Meriden, Conn.
w.c. 1810-1820, d. 1864

YALE & CURTIS
New York, N. Y.
1858-1867

YOULE, GEORGE
New York, N. Y.
w. 1793-1828

YOULE, THOMAS
New York, N. Y.
w. 1813-1819

YOUNG, ABRAHAM
New York, N. Y.
c. 1796

YOUNG, PETER
New York, N. Y.
c. 1775
Albany, N. Y.
w.c. 1785-*c.* 1800